NORTHERN CYPRUS

Windrush Island Guides
include

LANZAROTE
CORFU
MADEIRA and PORTO SANTO
MALTA, GOZO and COMINO
MENORCA
SARDINIA

THE AUTHORS   John and Margaret Goulding are experienced travel writers, and particularly fascinated by islands – they have already written guides to Lanzarote and Menorca for the Windrush Island Guides series. They live in West Sussex, where they have a bookselling business.

NORTHERN CYPRUS

John and Margaret Goulding

THE WINDRUSH PRESS
GLOUCESTERSHIRE

Acknowledgements

The authors gratefully acknowledge the help of the officers of the London representative of the Turkish Republic of North Cyprus, especially that of Mr Alper Faik Genç, press counsellor, and the tourism counsellor, Mr Özkan İrfanoğlu. Thanks are also due to the Gazimağusa tourist office; and to Mr Lemi Galip, Under-Secretary at the Ministry of Tourism in Lefkoşa, and Mr Mehmet Kiral, general manager of Cyprus Turkish Tourism Enterprises Ltd, both of whom supplied valuable guidance and encouragement and gave generously of their time. The International Council for Bird Preservation, Dee Darters, Peter (Bülent) Kneebone and Chris Cockshott, director of Dolphin Sailing, all assisted with particular sections of the book. Above all, we thank Timuçin Özbirim of Riverside Tatil Köyu, Alsancak, who never tired of our questions and was a mine of information on every subject.

First published in Great Britain by
The Windrush Press
Windrush House
Adlestrop, Moreton-in-Marsh
Gloucestershire
1992

Telephone: 0608 658075
Fax: 0608 658860

British Library Cataloguing in Publication Data
A catalogue record for this book is available from the
British Library

ISBN 0 900075 52 X

Typeset by DP Photosetting, Aylesbury, Bucks
Printed and bound in Hong Kong by Paramount Printing Group Ltd

Cover illustrations: (front) Monastery church of Panayia Absinthiotissa (back) Kantara Castle

CONTENTS

For the Özbirim family: Harper and Suna, Çağatay, Türkân and little Harper, Timuçin, İnanç and Enver

The Turkish Republic of North Cyprus

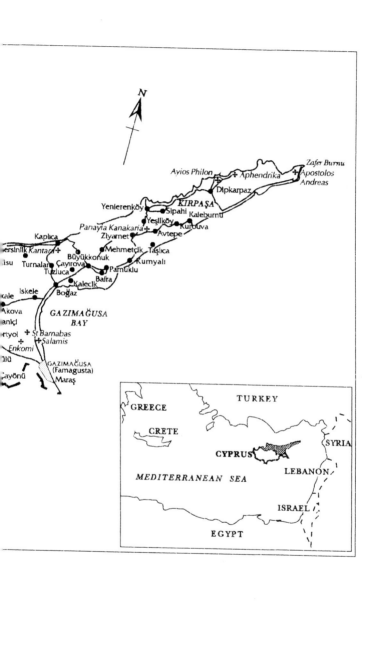

INTRODUCTION

Tourism in North Cyprus is still in its infancy. Its development has been hampered, no doubt, by the reluctance of the rest of the world to recognise the country's existence, and more recently by the Gulf War; but the slow speed of its growth (in marked contrast to the frenetic over-development which mars so much of the south of the island) is also partly intentional. The authorities recognise that in the 1990s their unspoilt beaches and undisfigured countryside have a rare value, and it is not proposed that the present 7,000-odd tourist beds should increase by more than a thousand or two.

As a result, North Cyprus offers all the pleasures promised by a Mediterranean holiday a generation ago, before mass tourism, high-rise hotels and a proliferation of concrete and fast food turned so many resorts into barely distinguishable clones of Benidorm. Experienced travellers return again and again, attracted by the lack of pressure and the easy pace of life, the beautiful beaches, stupendous scenery, reliable climate and the warmth of their hosts.

It is true that some of the cultural and sporting facilities to be found in many more developed holiday resorts are missing. There are few modern shops, European newspapers are hard to find and information is scanty in the museums and at historic sites. It is also true that, in some instances, the welcome extended to visitors coexists somewhat uneasily with the strong military presence perceived by the Republic as essential to maintain its security. But what North Cyprus lacks in sophistication it more than makes up for in courtesy and *joie de vivre*. The pace of life is slow and relaxing, and the genuine friendliness of the Cypriots is redolent of an earlier age. Visitors are treated as personal guests, and British holidaymakers in particular are disarmed, not only by the ubiquitous traces of past occupation (veteran pillar boxes with royal insignia, driving on the left, the nostalgia evoked by the numerous elderly British cars in the streets of Lefkoşa), but also by the extraordinary number of Cypriots who have lived in Britain at some time (or have relatives who still do) and will insist on reminiscing fondly about the old days over a *kahve* or a beer.

The scenery, always dominated by the romantic backdrop of the Beşparmak mountain range, is stunning, the beaches golden and practically empty, and the climate one of the most equable in the world. In contrast to the enormous hotels and crowded resorts of the more prosperous south, North Cyprus' resorts are sleepy and relaxing; there is no crime to speak of, the buildings are almost all on a human scale, the shopkeepers unpressing, and the restaurants leisurely and welcoming. Prices are low, too; gargantuan and delicious meals can be enjoyed for less than £5 a head and you can buy a bag of oranges almost too large to carry for 50p.

In addition to the beaches and the unrivalled scenery, the birds, butterflies and wild flowers of the island are glorious, particularly from February to May; there are excellent

View from the 'Queen's window', St Hilarion castle

opportunities for walking, painting and photography. Lovers of history, too, find much to fascinate them. Cyprus has been at the centre of the civilized world for most of her history and her soil bears the traces of every power down the ages which has ever sought to extend its influence in the eastern Mediterranean. There are Bronze Age sites to be explored, the spectacular ruins of classical Salamis and the fairy tale Crusader castles in the mountains: Greek temples, Roman theatres, Byzantine painted churches, flamboyant Gothic cathedrals and abbeys, Venetian fortifications, Ottoman mosques – North Cyprus has them all.

We hope this book will help you to enjoy the unique experience North Cyprus has to offer. *Hoş Geldiniz!*

GETTING THERE

By Air

Most visitors to North Cyprus book their holiday as a 'package', which has the advantage of avoiding the worry of arriving, late at night and after a long journey, with neither transport from Ercan airport nor an address to go to.

Tour operators offering holidays in North Cyprus include CTA Holidays, a subsidiary of the national carrier, Cyprus Turkish Airlines, 41 Pall Mall, London SW1Y 5JG (tel: 071 930 4953/4/5, fax: 071 930 1046); Celebrity Holidays, 18 Frith St, London W1V 5TS (tel: 071 734 4386, fax: 071 439 2026); Cricketer Holidays, 4 The White House, Beacon Road, Crowborough, East Sussex TN6 1AB (tel: 0892 664242, fax: 0892 662355); Metak Holidays, 70 Welbeck St, London W1M 7HA (tel: 071 935 6961, fax: 071 224 3675); Mosaic Holidays in conjunction with Noble Air, 73 South Audley St, London W1Y 5FF (tel: 071 355 3464, fax: 071 355 3750); President Holidays (who charter Istanbul Airlines), 17B Riding House St, London W1P 7PB (tel: 071 436 6447, fax: 071 636 7451); Regent Holidays, Regent House, 31A High St, Shanklin, Isle of Wight PO37 6JW (tel: 0983 864212/864225, fax: 0983 864197); Steep-west, 130–2 Wardour St, London W1V 3AU (tel: 071 629 2879, fax: 071 287 5377); and Sunquest, 9 Grand Parade, Green Lanes, London N4 1JX (tel: 081 800 8030, fax: 081 809 6629). All these holidays may be booked through local travel agents, and each company has representatives in the Republic to help you during your holiday.

It is perfectly simple, however, to concoct your own package by booking the accommodation of your choice and making independent travel arrangements, the only problem being that most European flights arrive quite late at night. The flight to North Cyprus (Ercan Airport) from the UK takes about six hours; a one-hour stop is always made in mainland Turkey, and this interruption will continue to be obligatory unless or until the TRNC achieves international recognition. Depending on the airline, the stop may be at Izmir or Istanbul ('two-centre' holidays featuring either city in addition to North Cyprus are widely available), but passengers for Ercan do not disembark until they reach their destination. Airlines operating flights between the UK and

All flights to North Cyprus make a stop-over in Turkey

North Cyprus are Cyprus Turkish Airlines, Istanbul Airlines and Noble Air, who all have daily flights. CTA's fare from the UK, in February 1992, was £86 single and £170 return (inc. tax). Independent travellers arriving from Turkey have a choice of flights from Istanbul, Ankara, Izmir, Antalya and Adana: any THY (Turkish Airlines) office or travel agent in Turkey will provide details.

Ercan airport, opened on 13 February 1975 to coincide with the establishment of North Cyprus as a Turkish federated state, is 15 miles (24 km) east of Lefkoşa (Nicosia), 23 miles (37 km) south of Girne (Kyrenia) and 32 miles (51 km) west of Gazimağusa (Famagusta). Formerly an RAF airfield, it was renamed to honour a pilot with the Turkish air force, Fehmi Ercan, who was killed at the age of 39 during the 1974 landings. He is commemorated as a martyr by a plaque behind the passport control booths in the departures area.

On arrival at Ercan, it is advisable to ask the immigration officers not to stamp your passport, as this will render any future visit to south Cyprus impossible and might also give rise to difficulties when entering Greece. Your request will meet with no surprise: the soldiers charged with laboriously typing your passport details into computer terminals on your arrival have separate visa forms available which they will endorse without question or comment.

Ercan airport is small and, as yet, inadequately equipped with trolleys or other facilities. A tourist information desk opens to coincide with flight arrivals and keeps a list of hotels, but there are no money-changing facilities. Car hire is available: there is no petrol station at the airport, but at night cars are filled with sufficient fuel to reach Gazimağusa, the furthest resort. No public transport runs from Ercan, but taxis meet all flights: establish the price for your destination before you set off (the driver must show you a tariff on request).

At the end of your visit, departure from Ercan is preceded by a lengthy bureaucratic process at passport control (have a pen ready to fill in a form); beyond this point, the departure lounge offers as much seating as its small size allows, two or three shops and a rather inadequate snack bar.

In 1986 a new civil airport was opened at Geçitkale, but it has been little used so far.

By Sea

Ferries to North Cyprus from Turkey run between Mersin and Gazimağusa, and between Taşucu (west of Silifke) and Girne. Both services are operated by Turkish Maritime Lines, Genel Mudurluk, Karaköy, Istanbul (tel: 01 433500), but are bookable from the UK through Sunquest Holidays (address p. 4). In the Republic, reservations may be made through most travel agencies in Girne or Gazimağusa or at Türk Bankası, 92 Girne Caddesi, Lefkoşa (tel: 020 71587). Sailings from Mersin are on Mondays, Wednesdays, Fridays and Sundays at 22.00 (spring 1992), arriving at Gazimağusa at 08.00 the next morning; and from Gazimağusa on Tuesdays, Thursdays and Saturdays at the same time. Single fares per person (inc. port tax) range from £28 for a reclining seat to £48 for a luxury cabin; cars are carried for £35 each way. An evening meal and breakfast are available on board. The ferry between Taşucu and Girne is much smaller, but operates in both directions on six days a week. It leaves Taşucu at midnight every day except Saturday, arriving in Girne at 08.00; departures from Girne (new harbour) are at 13.00 daily except Sundays, with arrival at Taşucu 4½ hours later. This ferry is for foot passengers only; there are no cabins and the single fare in spring 1992 was £15.

TRAVEL IN NORTH CYPRUS

Driving

Cypriots drive on the left and distances on road signs etc. are expressed in miles, a legacy of the British occupation. Currently the only significant dual carriageway is a stretch between Ercan airport and the outskirts of the capital, but North Cyprus has more metalled roads than the maps suggest. Few of them, however, have line markings, and the more minor roads are often narrow, necessitating putting one wheel onto the hard shoulder when meeting oncoming traffic. The use of front seatbelts is compulsory and young children must sit in the rear of the car. Within towns the speed limit is 30 mph (50 kmph), on the open road normally 60 (95) unless signs (often military) advise otherwise – note that the speedometers of hired cars may be in mph or kmph, depending on whether the vehicle is right- or left-hand drive.[1] In areas of military sensitivity you may meet signs forbidding stopping or photography, and by the entrances to some military camps drivers may be forced to slow down without much warning by a slalom of oil drums and barriers stretching halfway across the road. In the mountains and elsewhere away from the main centres there are a great number of rough tracks. It is usually perfectly safe to drive along these in a hired car, but care should be taken (especially in mountainous regions) if there has been recent rain, when surfaces may crumble and streams run down the track.

Visitors who bring their own car to North Cyprus receive a three-month permit, renewable three-monthly for up to a year, which exempts them from customs duty. Insurance valid in the TRNC is a requirement.

Road signs are international, but worded only in Turkish in most cases. Words worth learning in this connection are:

Dur	Stop
Dikkat	Attention
Girilmez	No entry
Yavaş	Slow
Azami Hiz	Maximum Speed

[1] For this reason distances are, wherever possible, expressed in both miles and km throughout this book.

Yol Yapim	Roadworks
Kücük araba	Small cars only (in parking spaces)
Askeri bölge	Military area
Yasak bölge	Forbidden zone
Fotograf Çekilmez	Photography not permitted
Yangin tehlikesı	Danger of fire.

Petrol prices are reasonable, at about 25 per cent less than in the UK, and stations are sufficiently frequent on the main routes. It is sensible, however, to keep your tank topped up as the opportunity occurs if you are driving any distance in the more remote corners of the north. Petrol stations usually close at 19.00 and do not open on Sundays. There is generally only one grade ('super') for sale; no unleaded petrol is yet available in the Republic.

Turkish Cypriots who can afford it love to own large BMWs and Mercedes, but often use these only around the towns, resorting to much older vehicles for excursions into the countryside. Particularly in the capital, lovers of British

Prohibitive red signs like this are still a familiar feature of the Republic's roads

cars of an earlier era will enjoy regular sightings of such nostalgic models as the Humber Super Snipe, Triumph Herald, Vauxhall Velox and 1950s Fords and Jaguars, all lovingly maintained.

Car Hire

All hire cars in North Cyprus are distinguished by red number plates and a Z prefix, an ingenious idea which encourages police and the military to show some indulgence to visitors; it does not, however, entitle the visitor to flout traffic regulations with impunity!

Most visitors to the Republic will want to hire a car for at least some of their stay and there are a number of agencies. Most rental cars are Renaults (9s or 12s), though Isuzu Geminis, Suzuki jeeps and a few other makes are also available: jeeps are a good idea for exploring the unmetalled roads, but think carefully before selecting one, as open-top drivers may not only get covered with dust but also risk an unexpected bout of sunstroke. A valid domestic driving licence is usually all that is required for car hire; some hirers insist on drivers being at least 25 years of age.

Typical car hire charges (1991) per day were:

Renault 12 TX (l.h.d.)	£7.50–£10.50
Renault 9 (r.h.d.)	£9.50–£13.50
Suzuki jeep or similar	£10.50–£17.50
Suzuki 7-seater jeep	£12.00–£20.00.

These prices included unlimited mileage and comprehensive insurance with an excess of £150, waivable by paying an extra £2 per day. Prices are at the lower end of this range in Nov–March and the higher in July–Sept. Most hirers quote for a minimum of three days and prices reduce slightly for hirings of more than eight days.

Car hire agencies in North Cyprus include: in Girne, Atlantic (office in the Dome Hotel, tel: 081 53053/52968, fax: 081 52772), Canlı Balık (38 Kordon Boyu, by the harbour, tel: 081 52182), Oscar (opposite the Dome, tel: 081 52272/53858, fax: 53858), Pacific Car Hire (23 Ecevit Cadd., tel: 081 52508) and Yeni Kartal (Denizkızı Kavşağı, Alsancak, tel: 082 18644). In Gazimağusa, Atlantic (Sinan Paşa Sok, tel: 036 63277), Deniz (Yeni Boğaziçi, near Salamis, tel: 036 65510) and Sur (Ismet Inönü Bulv., tel: 036 65600); and in Lefkoşa, Elite (103 Girne Cadd., tel: 020 73175), Sun (Abdi Ipekçi Cadd., tel: 020 78787) and Traveloz (Muzaffar Paşa Cadd., tel: 020 77147/71356). Some of these firms also have branches at Ercan airport.

A few bicycles and motorcycles are available for hire in

Girne and Gazimağusa. Tourist offices will provide details. Crash helmets must be worn by motorcyclists by law.

Taxis

Commonly luxurious Mercedes saloons, taxis display a yellow 'TAKSI' sign on the roof. They are only to be found at official ranks: they do not usually cruise around. Taxis are not metered, but there is an official tariff which the driver is obliged to show you on demand. It is always sensible to establish the fare for your proposed journey before setting out. Journeys between 24.00 and 06.00 are charged at a higher rate. The ranks in Lefkoşa are mostly in Atatürk Meydanı, the main square in the old city, where will be found (all telephone numbers prefixed by 020): Ankara (71788), Izmir (78242), NATO (72155), Özner (74012) and Yılmaz (73036). In Girne (telephone prefix 081) the Dome Taxi Service (at the hotel, tel: 52376) offers a 24-hour service. In Hürriyet Cadd., the main road through the town, are Güven (53172), Intur (52438) and Önder (52543); other ranks are Özgürel in Ecevit Cadd. (53610), Hız in Cengiz-kanlı Sok. (53552), and, in the harbour area, Jet (54943) and Liman Taxi (53395). In Gazimağusa (prefix 036), both Göçmen (62323) and Salamis (62200/62500) are based in Namık Kemal Meydanı outside the cathedral in the walled town; Istanbul Taxi (64464) is nearby in Istiklal Cadd., and Ömür Taxi at 2 Lala Mustafa Paşa Sok. (62233).

Dolmuşes (literally 'stuffed', because they only start when all the seats are full) are very reasonable shared taxis which follow specific routes between the main towns and villages. They are usually to be found at major bus stops.

Buses

Like Turkey, North Cyprus has an extensive network of bus routes linking many of the villages with their neighbours and with the main towns. Buses connecting Lefkoşa with Gazimağusa, Girne and Güzelyurt run up to three times an hour, and a through bus from Girne to Gazimağusa operates hourly on the half-hour. No strict timetable is adhered to, but the last bus in any direction may leave as early as 17.00, so it is advisable to check the return time on your outward journey. Fares are extremely cheap, e.g. less than 50p for a single journey from Girne to Lefkoşa.

Bus terminals are at 1 Ecevit Cadd. (beside the town hall and traffic lights) in Girne; on the main Lefkoşa road in the outskirts of Gazimağusa; between the Martyrs' Memorial and the Girne Gate in Lefkoşa and also on the corner of

Buses link most villages on North Cyprus with the main towns.

Mehmet Münir Mustafa and Doğan Cadd. on the road out towards Gazimağusa. On less busy routes, the service may be run by a minibus or *dolmuş*, or even a service taxi with a destination plate.

Designated stops (*otobus durak*) are easy to spot, but in rural areas buses will stop anywhere on request.

Maps

The AA/Macmillan Cyprus Traveller's map, widely available in the UK, is reasonably reliable and gives both Turkish and Greek place names for the North, which can be useful (though the Turkish name is given second). It is sometimes inaccurate, however, in its placing of the symbols marking archaeological and other sites of interest, and shows several roads which either do not exist or are impassable. Maps available on the island, giving Turkish place names only, are the ubiquitous tourist map (Kuzey Kıbrıs Turist Haritası), usually issued to car hirers, and the map of Cyprus published by K. Rüstem and Brother, P.O. Box 239, Lefkoşa, which includes good street plans of the three main cities.

HOTELS AND RESTAURANTS

Accommodation

Almost all visitors to North Cyprus stay in or near Girne or Gazimağusa. Hotels are graded by a 'star' system similar to that used by tourist authorities throughout Europe. All 'starred' hotels offer private WC, bath or shower rooms. Inflation in Turkey is high, so prices can alter frequently; nevertheless some establishments are willing to quote rates for up to six months ahead. Credit cards are widely accepted.

In general, accommodation is more expensive than in mainland Turkey, but appreciably cheaper than in most other Mediterranean holiday areas. Most hotels remain open throughout the year, as do the *pansiyons*, which offer clean but basic accommodation. It is usual for the price of breakfast to be included in the room rate.

The North Cyprus Tourist Office in London (*see p. 24*) has a list of the main hotels on the island, as do the tourist offices at Ercan airport, Girne and Gazimağusa. However, these offices do not handle reservations. To make an independent booking from outside North Cyprus, the telephone numbers in the list below should be prefixed by 905 and the '0' before the local code omitted. The abbreviations 'a-c' and 'c.h.' signify air-conditioning and central heating.

Hotels

GAZIMAĞUSA AREA

Palm Beach ★★★★★ south edge of city; a-c, c.h., pool, sandy beach, disco, casino, tennis, water sports, gymnasium, supermarket, souvenir shop, medical service, courtesy bus (tel: 036 62000/1, fax: 036 62002)
Park ★★★★ 7 miles (11 km) north; a-c, c.h., pool, private sandy beach, tennis, garden, water sports (tel: 036 65511/66511)
Salamis Bay ★★★★ 6 miles (9½ km) north; a-c, c.h., pool, private sandy beach, lift, tennis, garden, water sports, disco, casino (tel: 036 67201)
Boğaz ★★★ 16 miles (25½ km) north, in Boğaz; a-c, private

sandy beach (tel: 037 12559/12659) (*NB temporarily closed for restoration in summer 1991*)

Mimoza ★★★ 6 miles (9½ km) north; a-c, private sandy beach, tennis, water sports (tel: 036 67201)

Rebecca ★★★ 5½ miles (9 km) north; a-c, pool, garden (tel: 036 65803)

Sea View ★★★ 16 miles (25½ km) north, above Boğaz village; a-c, pool, garden, floodlit tennis (tel: 037 12651, fax: 020 82603)

Gıranel ★★ 11 miles (17½ km) north; on main road, but 2 minutes to beach, breakfast only (tel: 037 12455)

Altun Tabya ★ central Gazimağusa; a-c, evening meal on request (tel: 036 65363)

GIRNE AREA

Chateau Lambousa ★★★★★ 9 miles (14½ km) west; grandiose architecture, a-c, c.h., pool, tennis, 30 acres of gardens and citrus groves, conference facilities, courtesy bus to Girne (tel: 082 18751/2/3, fax: 082 18761)

Celebrity ★★★★ 9 miles (14½ km) west; a-c, c.h., pool, sandy beach, tennis, water sports, casino, underground disco, souvenir shop, courtesy bus to Girne (tel, fax: as Chateau Lambousa)

Dome ★★★★ old-established 'colonial' hotel in central Girne; a-c, c.h., seawater pool carved from the rock, rocky beach, lift, disco, casino (tel: 081 52453-7, fax: 020 52772)

Club Güzelyalı ★★★ 15 miles (24 km) west; c.h., sandy beach, garden (tel: 082 18996)

Club Kyrenia ★★★ 2 miles (3 km) east; a-c, c.h., pool, rocky beach, water sports, courtesy bus to Girne (tel: 081 54801/52363, fax: 081 53858)

Denizkızı ★★★ 6 miles (9½ km) west; a-c, c.h., private sandy cove, water sports, lift, children's playground (tel: 082 18710, fax: 082 18433)

Dorana ★★★ town centre, 300 yds (300 m) from sea; a-c, c.h., lift, local cuisine (tel: 081 53521/2)

Grand Rock ★★★ central; a-c, c.h., pool, rocky beach, disco, casino (tel: 081 52238/52379)

Liman ★★★ overlooking yacht harbour; a-c, lift, casino (tel: 081 52001, fax: 081 52002)

Mare Monte ★★★ 7 miles (11 km) west; a-c, c.h., private sandy beach, water sports, tennis, riding, disco (tel: 082 18310/2)

Anadol ★★ town centre; a-c, lift, garden, children's playground (tel: 081 52319)

Atlantis ★★ beside yacht harbour with views to castle; a-c, lift (tel: 081 52242/52505)

British ★★ (formerly Ergenekon), by yacht harbour (tel: 081 52240, fax: 081 52742)

Golden Bay ★★ 6 miles (9½ km) west; a–c, local cuisine (tel: 082 18630)

Marmaris ★★ 9 miles (14½ km) west; rocky beach, restaurant overlooking sea (tel: 082 18575)

Socrates ★★ town centre; garden, Turkish cuisine (tel: 081 52157, fax: 081 51293)

Bristol ★ in main street; garden, Turkish cuisine (tel: 081 52298)

Both Girne and Gazimağusa have *pansiyon* accommodation to suit the traveller on a budget. Addresses and telephone numbers may be obtained from the local tourist offices (*see p. 24*). The **Courtyard Inn** at Karakum (tel: 081 53343) is especially attractive: it has five rooms and a superior outdoor restaurant. Bed and breakfast in 1991 was £15 per person in summer and £10 in winter. Clinging to the steep hillside above Lapta, **Lapta Gardens**, a delightful converted house with a swimming pool, offers bed and breakfast, with air-conditioning and heating, for 12 people. It can be booked through President Holidays (*see p. 4*).

On the Kirpaşa peninsula, 3 miles (5 km) south-east of Dipkarpaz, the 5-roomed **Blue Sea Hotel** overlooks a small harbour and a sandy beach. The price of a room in summer 1991 was £11 per night, with half-board available. There are also a handful of small *pansiyons* which offer simple accommodation along this road, such as the **Golden Beach** (restaurant and 2 rooms), which stands by an attractive south-facing beach.

LEFKOŞA

Saray ★★★ Atatürk Meydanı; a–c, c.h., lift, rooftop restaurant, casino, under the same management as the Dome in Girne (tel: 020 71115, fax: 020 52772)

There are several *pansiyons* in the old part of the city, and, outside the walls, the **Ender Pansiyon**, 12 Şehit Ismail Dümenci Sok., Yenişehir (tel: 020 78612/78506, fax: 020 78673). Another possibility is the **Demerka Hotel**, Gazeteci Kemal Aşik Cadd. (tel: 020 83406).

Self-Catering

As eating out in North Cyprus is cheap and interesting, many visitors prefer to stay in villas or apartments. North Cyprus offers a wide choice of this type of accommodation: a group of units is often called a *tatil köyü* (holiday village).

Standards are generally high and many developments have an excellent range of attendant facilities: restaurants, water sports, children's play areas, etc. If there is a restaurant, the basic tariff may include the price of breakfast.

Jasmine Court (5-star) and **Girne View** (4-star) are 'aparthotels', with 'star' grading; they combine the features of a hotel with superior self-catering apartments. Other complexes, many of which are excellent, are not graded in this way.

Most establishments are open all the year round.

GAZIMAĞUSA AREA

Cyprus Gardens, $11\frac{1}{2}$ miles ($18\frac{1}{2}$ km) north (signed from Ercan airport); opened 1989, very secluded, a-c, c.h., pool, sandy beach, water sports, tennis, horse riding, mini-market (tel: 037 12552/12722, fax: 020 83739)

Dağli Aparthotel, 6 miles ($9\frac{1}{2}$ km) north; opened 1989, a-c, lift, 5 minutes' walk to sandy beach (tel: 036 67864)

Khan Aparthotel, outskirts of city, on Salamis road; above restaurant (tel: 036 66999)

Laguna Beach Aparthotel, next to Palm Beach Hotel; a-c, sandy beach, lift (tel: 036 66502/3)

Long Beach Bungalows, $10\frac{1}{2}$ miles (17 km) north; sandy beach, very large restaurant, wind-surfing, table tennis (tel: 037 88282)

Salamis Bay Complex, 6 miles ($9\frac{1}{2}$ km) north; bungalows and apartments alongside large hotel; a-c (except Garden Apartments), pool, sandy beach, supermarket; facilities, including water sports, shared with hotel (tel: 036 67201/6)

Yakal Aparthotel 11 miles ($17\frac{1}{2}$ km) north; on main road but within easy reach of a sandy beach (tel: 037 12724)

GIRNE AREA

Ambelia Village, 4 miles ($6\frac{1}{2}$ km) south-east, above Bellapais; a-c, pool, garden, 1,000 feet (300 m) above sea level (tel: 081 52175)

Celebrity Bungalows, 9 miles ($14\frac{1}{2}$ km) west; a-c, c.h., pool, sandy beach, sports facilities, tennis, casino and disco shared with sister hotel (tel: 082 18751/2/3, fax: 082 18761)

Club Acapulco, 7 miles (11 km) east; a-c, pool, sandy beach, mature gardens, tennis, basketball, water sports, children's playground, bus to Girne (tel: 081 53510/1, fax: 081 53870)

Club Lapethos, 9 miles ($14\frac{1}{2}$ km) west; opened 1990, c.h., pool, sandy beach, underground disco (tel: 082 18961)

Girne View south on the Lefkoşa road, a-c, c.h., lift, garden, transport to harbour and beaches, supermarket, souvenir shop (tel: 081 54989, fax: 081 54407) (*NB temporarily closed summer 1991*)

Green Olives, 4 miles (6½ km) east, in Çatalköy; a-c, garden, 10-minute walk to sea (tel: 081 53878)

Jasmine Court, 2 miles (3 km) west, opened 1990; extensive landscaped grounds, rocky beach, a-c, c.h., lift, pool, tennis, gymnasium, children's playground, supermarket (tel: 081 51450, fax: 081 51489)

L.A. Holiday Centre, 9 miles (14½ km) west; opened 1990, a-c, pool, private sandy beach, water sports, tennis, gift shop, courtesy bus to Girne (tel: 082 18981, fax: 082 18992)

Olive Tree, 5 miles (8 km) east, in Çatalköy; a-c, c.h., pool, tennis, courtesy bus to Girne (tel: 084 14200)

Riverside, 8 miles (13 km) west, in Alsancak, 1½ miles (2½ km) inland; a-c, c.h., pool, lovely gardens, tennis, high standards, friendly atmosphere and very peaceful (tel: 082 18906/7, fax: 082 18908)

Riviera Bungalows, 3 miles (5 km) west, in Karaoğlanoğlu; a-c, bungalows by rocky beach (tel: 081 53369)

Şerif Hotel Apartments, 2 miles (3 km) west, a-c, lift (tel: 081 54782)

Silver Waves Hotel Apartments, 4 miles (6 km) west, in Karaoğlanoğlu; a-c, c.h., sandy beach (tel: 081 53480)

Top Set Bungalows, 5 miles (8 km) west, in Karaoğlanoğlu; a-c, c.h., pool, sandy beach (tel: 081 52890)

Villa Club, 5 miles (8 km) west, in 10 acres of citrus groves; pool, 8 minutes' walk to beach (tel: 082 18400)

Camping

As yet there are only two purpose-built camp sites in North Cyprus: **Riviera Bungalows** (tel: 081 53369), 3 miles (5 km) west of Girne, and **Onur Camping** (tel: 037 65314), 5 miles (8 km) north of the Salamis Bay Hotel on Gazimağusa bay. Both offer a site beside the sea. Riviera Bungalows has small chalets to let as well as space for tents. Here the shoreline is predominantly rocky. Restaurant facilities are at hand in both cases. Onur Camping is set among the pines by a long golden beach; its restaurant serves excellent food and offers live music and dancing on Saturdays.

At Neşe Plaj, on the southern perimeter of Boğaz, there is camping at the water's edge. On the Kirpaşa peninsula, small sites adjoin the restaurant and sandy beaches of Yenierenköy Halk Plaj (public beach) and Teresa Plaj, north-east of Yenierenköy. Informal camping may well be permissible elsewhere, but it is always advisable to enquire locally before pitching a tent.

Cypriot Cuisine

Although the cuisine of North Cyprus has a strong Turkish accent, it has its own distinct specialities. For example, the addition of lemon juice to *hummus* (chickpea and tahini paste) is characteristically Cypriot; lemon, in fact, is a favourite flavouring for sweet and savoury dishes.

As in Turkey, the **mezes** are the most important part of a meal. Ostensibly they are *hors d'oeuvres* but so numerous, imaginative and filling that they can quite easily constitute a whole meal. On occasions, so many portions are presented that you may feel the need to equip yourself with a 'doggy bag'.

Typical cold *mezes* are: *tarama*, a paste made from spiced cod roe; *taltur* or *cacık*, yogurt with cucumber and dill; fried courgettes; fried aubergines; *pilaki*, red or white beans; stuffed green peppers; raw carrot in lemon juice; runner beans in tomato sauce; *dolma*, vine leaves stuffed with meat, rice or pickled vegetables; tomatoes and onions in hot chili sauce; and *hummus* with lemon. Supplementary small dishes

Preparing the *mezes* at the Paradise Restaurant

of plain yogurt, black olives, hard-boiled egg, *beyaz peynir* (white cheese made from sheep's milk) and vegetables in mayonnaise are also placed on the table at this stage. The secret is not to rush; as the cold *mezes* disappear they are replaced by a smaller selection of hot delicacies. These will probably include *hellim*, the goats' cheese of Cyprus, grilled or fried: the texture is slightly rubbery but the flavour delicious. A home-made piquant lamb sausage typical of Cyprus (*şeftali*), spiced or unspiced *köfte* (meat rissoles) and battered *kalamares* (baby squid) may all be brought piping hot. You may also be offered *böreks*, slender tubes of *fyllo* pastry, filled with cheese, minced lamb or spinach. Boiled or roasted snails are a speciality of the Kırpaşa peninsula.

Main courses tend to be less elaborate concoctions. *Kebabs* (*kebaps*) are very popular: cubes of tender lamb, chicken, liver or fish are skewered with onion and peppers, grilled over charcoal and served on a bed of rice or with envelopes of pitta bread; this will certainly be accompanied by salad. *Tava* is a casserole of lamb, onion and herbs served in its baking dish; *musakka*, as in Greece, is minced lamb with aubergines and *béchamel* sauce; *pirohu* is similar to ravioli, the pasta parcels containing cheese and mint. On feast days or in ethnic restaurants you may have the chance to sample *kup kebabı*: chunks of lamb are wrapped in foil, together with potatoes, onions and tomatoes, and baked for 2–3 hours in a brick or clay oven, sometimes underground. The origins of this dish are obscure, but it is said that the subterranean cooking, which emits no smells, enabled Turkish Cypriot villagers to cook a feast in secrecy, thereby avoiding a multitude of uninvited guests!

Fish is always an option on seaside menus and is very fresh. Mediterranean species often have no English name. e.g. *lahos* and *mercan*. Translatable varieties include *barbun* (red mullet), *kefal* (grey mullet), *palamut* (tuna), *sorgo* (white bream), *fagri* (sea bream), *beyaz* (sea bass) and *mineri* (amberjack). French fries and salad are the usual accompaniments.

In common with other Middle Eastern people, the Turkish Cypriot has a sweet tooth; this is reflected in the **desserts** on offer. *Lokma* are small balls of flour, sugar and yeast, fried, dipped in syrup and served hot; *helva* is a pudding made with semolina and pine-nuts; *sütlâc* is reminiscent of baked custard but uses ground rice; *kadayif* has the texture of shredded wheat and is saturated with syrup, and *baklava* is a light pastry filled with walnuts and drenched with lemon-flavoured syrup after baking. Fresh fruit (*mehve*) and ice cream (*dondurma*) are usually available as alternatives to these very sweet confections. The main towns have pastry shops where cakes, sweets, biscuits and Turkish delight (*lokum*) may be eaten with a cup of tea or coffee or taken away in boxes. **Petek Pastanelerı** near the Sea Gate in Gazimağusa is an attractive example, as is the **Akpinar** in Girne.

Coffee houses are a part of Turkish Cypriot life and are patronised almost exclusively by men who meet to talk and play backgammon. Turkish **coffee** (*kahve*) is strong and an acquired taste: you will be asked if you want it *sade* (without sugar), *orta* (medium-sweet) or *şekerli* (sweet). It is not served with milk but with an accompanying glass of water. If you would like milk in your coffee, ask for 'Nescafé' – here a generic term. Tea (*çay*), pronounced 'Chai', is also served without milk and usually in a glass rather than a cup.

Refreshing non-alcoholic drinks include fresh orange or lemon juice, sour cherry juice and *ayran*, lightly salted yogurt diluted with water and ice. Although mineral water is widely on sale, the tap water on North Cyprus is generally safe and good to drink, particularly in the Girne area. Around Gazimağusa it can taste salty after a dry summer.

Turkish Cypriots often drink *rakı*, the national drink of Turkey, with their *mezes*. This is a potent aniseed spirit which turns cloudy when diluted with water. Most holiday-makers prefer *rakı* as an aperitif; alternatively 'brandy sour', which is the local brandy (Safa or Antik) mixed with bitters and lemonade, garnished with orange or lemon and served in a glass with a sugared rim. Beer is a palatable light lager imported from Turkey.

All **wine** served in restaurants comes from Turkey and is good value. North Cyprus' own wines, Aphrodite and Kantara, both made in small quantities from grapes grown on the Kirpaşa, are considered inferior and only used in blended table wines; a sherry called Monarch is also made from these grapes. Red wines include Dikmen and Külüp from Central Anatolia, Villa Doluça (a blend of Anatolian wines), Karmen (heavy and dark), Yakut with a very pleasant and distinctive bouquet, and Papskarası which resembles Chianti. Readily available white wines are Villa Doluça, Vadi, Çankaya, Nevşehir, Sungurlu, Agora and Elysia. The sparkling dry Diren is usually drunk as an aperitif. Most international liqueurs are on sale at bars and restaurants.

Restaurants

A wide choice of restaurants in the main tourism centres gives the visitor a chance to eat somewhere different every night. Most restaurateurs and their staff are friendly and welcoming, and service is invariably attentive. During the summer months eating is often out of doors. As in western Europe, lunch is usually taken between 12.00 and 14.30 and dinner between 19.30 and 22.30 – at weekends, especially, when all Cypriots seem to eat out, restaurants are quite prepared for guests arriving well after 22.00. Cafeterias and some restaurants serve snacks throughout the day. Children are always made welcome – Turkish Cypriots invariably take them along when they eat out, however late the hour.

International foods – steak, pizza, chicken, salads etc. – are easy to find, but most establishments pride themselves on their *mezes* (*see p. 17*) and kebabs. The Turkish dishes usually represent the best value on any menu.

GIRNE

Canlı Balık, by the harbour; fresh fish, *mezes*, open 09.00–02.00 all year, also offers car hire (tel: 081 52182)

Grapevine, on the Lefkoşa road; international cuisine, popular with 'ex-pats' at lunchtimes; open 11.00–24.00 except Sun. (tel: 081 52496)

Harbour Club, next to the castle; French-style cuisine; booking advisable, expensive; open 11.00–24.00 except Tues. (tel: 081 52211)

Niazi's, opposite the Dome Hotel; famous for kebabs; established in Limassol 1949; open 17.00–23.00 except Weds., but serves lunch in winter (tel: 081 52160)

Papillon, on Lefkoşa road; live music, expensive; open 19.30–24.00 except Mon. (tel: 081 52355)

The unpretentious Perge restaurant, Girne, perches above some ancient rock-cut tombs

Perge, above the Roman tombs opposite the Icon Museum; home cooking, unassuming and very cheap (tel: 081 54629)

Set, by the harbour; fish restaurant, reasonable; open 10.00–24.00 (tel: 081 52336)

Tepebaşı, Nurettin Ersin Cadd.; no choice, traditional 'full kebab' dinner of several courses; high quality food and quick service, very popular with locals and extremely reasonable, with an outdoor terrace giving a view over the whole of Girne; perhaps the best 'authentic' eating in town, but a little hard to find: follow blue signs from Girne bypass through a housing estate; open 18.00–24.00 except Tues. (tel: 081 52380)

WEST OF GIRNE

Ali Paşa, Lapta, on the main road and fronting the sea; run by the 'Basil Fawlty' of North Cyprus, who will greet you with uproarious insults when he knows you; no menu, but good food; live music and dancing at weekends, when the place gets very full; snooker table (tel: 082 18515)

Altınkaya, 5 miles west, overlooking Yavuz Çikarma Plaj, by Peace and Freedom monument; excellent fish restaurant, very popular, especially at weekends (tel: 082 18341)

Başpinar, Lapta, high on the mountainside above the village; wonderful views (tel: 082 18661)

Duckworth House, Karaman, off the road below the village; Ian and Linda Smith, committed members of a new wave of British settlers, serve morning coffee, English lunches and dinners, afternoon tea; very homely with a pretty garden and swimming pool, closed Thurs. (tel: 081 52880)

Gazino, Alsancak, by the beach east of the military camp; run by soldiers, children's playground, reasonable prices

L.A. Holiday Centre, Lapta, large octagonal glass restaurant overlooking its beach; attentive service, exceptional *mezes*, live music (tel: 082 18981)

Rita on the Rocks, Lapta, small restaurant with outdoor seating by circular pool; Rita (British) is an effervescent host, Ergün, her Cypriot husband, a very good cook; Cypriot and international cuisine; popular with ex-pats (no telephone at the time of writing)

Treasure, Karaman, former Greek school; glorious views; Turkish and European food, reasonable prices (no telephone)

EAST OF GIRNE

Abbey House, Bellapais, in a converted Cypriot house

Sophisticated dining at the Courtyard Inn

with jasmine-scented walled garden close to the abbey; candle-lit dinners, French cuisine, booking advisable, expensive, open all year 19.30–24.00 except Sun. (tel: 081 53460)

Courtyard Inn, Karakum, 1½ miles (2½ km) east of Girne; jointly owned by two European couples; French-style cuisine in delightful courtyard garden; open all year for lunch and dinner; five bed and breakfast rooms available (tel: 081 53343)

Lemon Tree, Karakum, on the main road; small rural house, very friendly, fresh fish a speciality (tel: 081 54845)

Old Mill, Ozanköy, converted olive press near village mosque; good cheap Cypriot food cooked by the owner (no telephone)

Paradise Restaurant, Çatalköy, off main road 3 miles from Girne; owner/chef Ahmet Derviş had a restaurant in Chiswick for many years – a Gibbard cartoon bemoaning his departure hangs in the Paradise; imaginative *mezes*, using local cheese and yogurt; no set menu, friendly atmosphere; live music and crowds on Sats, when it is packed; very reasonable (tel: 081 52356)

Zia's, Çatalköy, on southern perimeter of the village; fish restaurant, popular with locals and very reasonable; live music; open all year 12.00–24.00 (tel: 081 52927)

GAZIMAĞUSA

Agora, 17 Elmas Tabya Sok.; ethnic Turkish-Cypriot restaurant specializing in *kup kebabi* (*see p. 18*), cooked in mud ovens in the street outside; fresh farm yogurt; open 09.00–24.00 except Sun. (tel: 036 65364)

Cyprus House, Polat Paşa Bulvari (opp. Telecommunications Office); in the garden of the old British police station; tables interspersed with classical relics; private collection of paintings, textiles, pottery and furniture on view in adjoining rooms; friendly atmosphere, occasional belly dancer; reasonable; open 12.00–15.00 and 18.00–02.00 except Sun. (tel: 036 64845)

La Cheminée, 17 Kemal Server Sok., opposite Palm Beach Hotel; French management, ambience and cuisine; seafood flown in from Europe; attentive service, expensive; open 12.00–14.00 and 19.30–22.30 except Mon. (tel: 036 64624)

Viyana, Yeşil Deniz Sok.; kebab restaurant a few doors down from Petek's pastry shop; attractive shady garden.

NORTH OF GAZIMAĞUSA

Akdeniz, just north of entrance to Salamis Bay Hotel

Çarli's, Boğaz, on the beach and overlooking fishing harbour; lively atmosphere, locally caught fish, very cheap; open 09.00–23.00 (tel: 037 12515)

Karsel, Boğaz, next door to Çarli's; popular fish restaurant, with a platter of fresh fish brought to the table to choose from; reasonable prices

Kocareis, on the beach beside Mimoza Hotel; limited menu, always busy; live music and stunning transvestite belly dancer on Fridays; very cheap (tel: 037 12620)

Onur, on the beach opposite the Gıranel Hotel, attached to small campsite; very friendly atmosphere; good Turkish-Cypriot food at reasonable prices; live music and dancing on Saturdays (tel: 037 65314)

LEFKOŞA

Annibal, traditional kebab house in the eastern part of the old city

Çağlayan, popular restaurant outside the walls, off the Gazimağusa road

Saray Hotel, Atatürk Square; rooftop restaurant with open terrace affording views all over Lefkoşa, north and south; open for lunch and dinner all year (tel: 020 71115)

PRACTICAL INFORMATION

Tourist Offices

The TRNC has a tourist office in London at 28 Cockspur St, SW1 5BN (tel: 071 930 5069, fax: 071 839 5282). The Tourism Counsellor, Mr Özkan İrfanoğlu, can provide colourful tourist booklets and maps in advance of your visit. Although he does not book accommodation, he has lists of hotels and self-catering complexes, and his office is open 09.30–17.30, Monday to Friday. As yet the TRNC has no other overseas tourist offices.

In North Cyprus itself there are tourist offices at Ercan airport (tel: 023 14737), in Lefkoşa and in the two resorts of Girne and Gazimağusa. The Lefkoşa office is currently housed within the Ministry of Tourism (tel: 020 75052/3), though there are plans to resite it in the upper chamber of the Girne Gate, which would certainly be more convenient for visitors to the city. In Girne the tourist information office is easily found beside the old harbour (30 Kordon Boyu, tel: 081 52145); in Gazimağusa it is outside the southern wall of the old city at 5 Fevzi Çakmak Cadd. (tel: 036 62864). Opening hours are: mid-May to late Sept, Tuesday to Friday 07.30–14.00 (Mondays 15.30–18.00 also); Oct–early May, 08.00–13.00 and 14.00–17.00.

Time

For most of the year, Cypriot time is 2 hours ahead of GMT. However, summer time ends during the last week-end of September, so during October Cyprus is only one hour ahead.

Banks and Currency

Numerous Turkish and Turkish Cypriot banks operate in North Cyprus. They open from Monday to Saturday at 08.30 (except public holidays); closing time in summer may be as early as 12.00 noon, but in winter most banks reopen from 14.00–17.00 on at least two days of the week. Banks will cash British cheques on production of a cheque card, but they charge commission for this and any other transaction.

For changing cash or travellers' cheques it is probably preferable to go to a money exchange. These open from 08.00–13.00 and 14.30–18.00 Monday to Friday (08.00–13.00 on Saturdays). Not only do they give a slightly better rate than the banks, but they may not charge commission. The reception desks at most hotels and villa complexes are usually very happy to change money; they study the daily paper for the going rate.

The monetary unit in North Cyprus is the Turkish lira (TL), which is a rapidly devaluing currency.[1] In consequence, restaurant and other prices may change frequently and prices for excursions, car hire, expensive souvenirs and imported goods may be quoted in foreign currency; it is sensible for visitors not to change more of their money into the local currency than is required for immediate needs, since the exchange rate may well improve several times during the course of a visit.

Credit cards are accepted in many restaurants and tourist shops; they are not, however, usable at petrol stations. Eurocheques are not very useful in North Cyprus.

Public Holidays

During the year North Cyprus has nine public holidays:

1 January	New Year's Day
23 April	Children's Day (designated by Atatürk and also known as National Sovereignty Day)
1 May	Labour Day
19 May	Youth and Sports Day (Youth Bayram)
20 July	Peace and Freedom Day (the anniversary of the landing of Turkish troops at Karaoğlanoğlu in 1974)
1 August	Communal Resistance Day (in fact the anniversary of the Ottoman conquest of Famagusta in 1571; also known as TMT day, honouring the Turkish Cypriot resistance movement)
30 August	Victory Day
29 October	Turkish National Day
15 November	Independence Day (proclamation of the TRNC)

[1] For this reason, where prices are given in this book they are usually expressed in pounds sterling.

In addition to these are the religious holidays, which follow the Muslim calendar: they are thus ten days earlier each year.

Şeker or *Ramazan Bayram* three days of feasting and celebration ending the 30-day fast of Ramadan (*şeker* means sugar); in 1992 this festival was 4–6 April

Kurban Bayram four days during which lambs are traditionally sacrificed and shared with the poor (11–14 June in 1992)

Mevlûd Mohammed's birthday (8 September in 1992)

These religious holidays are marked by exchanging gifts, eating special meals, playing music and visiting friends and relations. Foreign visitors to the island are welcome to join in the celebrations.

Post

In February 1992, the postage to Europe was 1150 TL for a card and 1500 TL for a letter; delivery times are excellent – usually 4–7 days after posting. When addressing a letter to the TRNC the code 'Mersin 10, Turkey' should follow the name of the town. If 'North Cyprus' appears on the envelope, the letter is likely to be misdirected to the south, possibly irretrievably. Stamps (*pul*) for postcards may be on sale alongside the cards (which cost around 2000 TL each and are, it must be said, generally of the direst quality).

Post Offices (*Posta Diaresi*) can be found, in Girne, on the left of the main road east towards Çatalköy (Cumhuriyet Cadd.); in Gazimağusa, inside the Land Gate ravelin at the south-west corner of the old walls and in Ilker Karter Cadd., one block east of Polat Paşa Bulv.; in Lefkoşa, in Sarayönü Sok. off Atatürk Meydanı and at Kaynaklı 1, Kızılay Sok; and in Güzelyurt, in Kurtuluş Sok. Opening hours are 08.00–13.00 and 14.00–17.00 (09.00–12.00 on Saturdays).

Philately is popular in North Cyprus, and packets of stamps are widely on sale in the shops. New issues are frequent and main post offices have philatelic counters. Further information is available from the Directorate of the Postal Department, Philatelic Branch, Lefkoşa.

Telephones

Telephone calls may be made from telecommunications offices, kiosks and the reception desks of hotels and villa complexes; there is direct dialling to 85 countries. In modern public call boxes (not the nostalgic British-installed booths complete with buttons A and B often seen, which although still standing are no longer in use), *cetones* are used

Most post boxes date from colonial days, but since 1974 the British-installed telephone kiosks have been superseded

in place of coins: these are obtainable at a nearby kiosk or shop and three different denominations are sold. For overseas calls, dial the international code (0044 for the UK, for example, 00353 for Ireland, 001 for the USA, 0049 for Germany and 0061 for Australia); then the number you are calling minus the initial zero of the area code. There is no off-peak rate; in September 1991 a one-minute call to the UK cost approximately £1.25. (To call North Cyprus from the UK dial 010 905, then the rest of the number, omitting the initial zero.)

Telephone codes in North Cyprus are 020 for Lefkoşa, 081 and 082 for Girne and district, 036 and 037 for Gazimağusa and district, 071 for Güzelyurt and 078 for Lefke.

Increasing numbers of hotels and businesses now have fax machines.

Health and Medical Care

Visitors receive free emergency medical treatment at State Hospitals, but not from individual doctors. Receipts for medical services and any prescribed medicines should be obtained to support any claim on a holiday medical insurance policy, and taking out some such policy is to be recommended. All blood used in hospitals is screened for AIDS.

Pharmacists (*Eczane*) can give qualified medical advice and can dispense many medicines over the counter. They are generally open from 08.00–18.00 Monday to Saturday, and outside these hours a rota system ensures that one pharmacist in each area is open 24 hours and on Sundays: there should be a notice on the door giving its location.

The Lefkoşa Burhan Nalbantoğlu Hospital is on the Girne road, just south of the major roundabout with a triumphal monument as you approach the capital (tel: 020 71441-51). There is also a Poliklinik (Health Centre) in the city on the main road out to Gazimağusa at Kızılay Sok. (tel: 020 73996). Girne's Akçiçek Hospital is in Cumhuriyet Cadd., east of the centre (tel: 081 52266); Gazimağusa's in Polat Paşa Bulv., just south of the walled city (tel: 036 62876). There is a fourth hospital, the Cengiz Topel, by the golf course at Yeşilyurt (tel: 077 17351). All these operate ambulances, reachable on the telephone numbers given. In addition there are local health centres in Akdoğan, Esentepe, Geçitkale, Güzelyurt, Iskele, Lapta, Lefke and Yenierenköy.

If a general practitioner is required, Dr Sait Kenan practises at 7 Osman Paşa Cadd. in Lefkoşa (tel: 020 73513); in Girne Dr Hakan Atakur has a clinic (open 09.00–12.30, 15.00–18.00, Mon–Fri) at 101 Kordon Apt, opposite the Dome Hotel (tel: 081 52065), or treatment may be sought from Dr Salih Miroğlu (also an MP), 75 Namık Kemal Cadd. (tel: 081 53577); in Gazimağusa, Dr Aytekin Çolakoğlu is at 2 Afrodit Sok. (tel: 036 62616) and Dr Ahmet Kirişoğlu at 15 Ağustos Bulv., 34 (036 65342). Dentists are also available in all three cities: in Lefkoşa Mr Erdoğan Mirata, 1 Osman Paşa Cadd. (tel: 020 72072); in Girne, Mr Kuydul Turan, 101 Kordon Apt (tel: 081 52065); and in Gazimağusa, Mr Fehmi Tunce, 3 Naim Efendi Yolu (tel: 036 63001/64896).

SUNSTROKE

From May until September the sun is extremely hot and care should be taken to avoid over-exposing the body or taking excessive exercise during the hottest part of the day. Cyprus' latitude means that the sun is higher in the sky than in many parts of the Mediterranean and a sunhat should be worn as protection for the head and neck. Extra awareness is especially appropriate when driving in an open-topped vehicle: a cooling breeze is deceptive and provides no protection against sunstroke. Symptoms are headaches, nausea, lassitude, sweating, cramps (due to the loss of salt) and rapid heartbeat. If affected, sponging with cold water and drinking salted water will assist recovery.

SNAKEBITES

It is unlikely that you will be bitten, as the snakes of North Cyprus are not aggressive. However, the recommended treatment for a bite is to apply a tourniquet between the wound and the heart, then to seek medical help. A doctor will administer an antibiotic. If possible, snakebite victims should either stay where they are or be carried to a source of treatment, since movement encourages the venom to spread throughout the body.

Water

The tap water of North Cyprus is generally safe to drink and, in the mountain areas, is very good. However the recent series of dry winters have left the reservoirs low in the Girne and Gazimağusa areas, and around the latter the water can taste disagreeably saline. Many holidaymakers prefer to drink bottled mineral water and this is freely available at very little cost.

Lavatories

Public conveniences are few and far between, and it is perfectly acceptable to use the facilities in hotels and restaurants. In Girne, the Dome Hotel's lavatories are immediately to the left after going through the main door; in Lefkoşa, the Saray Hotel's adjoin the restaurant on the top floor; in Gazimağusa there are convenient lavatories at Petek Pastaneleri, just inside the door on the left.

Beaches which make a charge for their facilities usually have lavatories, as do those with restaurants behind them.

Tipping

It is normal for a service charge of 10 per cent to be added to a restaurant bill and not necessary to leave any further gratuity. If the food or service has been exceptional, however, a small additional tip is always appreciated. Taxi-drivers, hair-dressers etc. resemble their counterparts everywhere else in the world in their attitude to the subject.

Electricity

A new power station is under construction east of Lara Beach, which will solve the Republic's present problems in this respect; completion is scheduled for 1993. Until then, electricity is imported from the south of the island, and overloading of the system has produced the inconvenience of fairly regular power cuts throughout the Republic; these tend to occur in the early evening. Much of the tourist accommodation, however, has emergency generators to cope with the problem.

Electrical sockets are usually of the 3-pin British type and the current is 240/415 volts AC.

Newspapers, Radio and Television

Unlike many Mediterranean holiday islands, North Cyprus does not have an abundant supply of English, American or German newspapers for sale. Prior to the difficulties experienced by Polly Peck International, the *Cyprus Times* was published in English each Friday; now its appearance is very sporadic. Turkish national newspapers and magazines crowd the news-stands, but North Cyprus also has its own: *Halkin Sesi* (*Voice of the People*, owned by the son of Dr Fazıl Küçük), *Birlik* (*Unity*), *Kıbrıs Postası* (*Cyprus Post*) and *Kıbrıs Gazetesı* (*Cyprus Gazette*) are dailies; *Yenigon* is weekly. The Public Information Office issues a free paper, *Kıbrıs*, monthly for the benefit of English-speaking residents and visitors: it may be found at hotel reception desks.

The BBC World Service can be heard in North Cyprus on various frequencies at different times of day: 17.64 MHz from 08.00–16.15 (GMT) and 15.07 MHz from 06.00–17.15 are the main frequencies. Also worth trying are 9.66 MHz from 09.00–15.15, 9.41 MHz from 04.00–07.30 and 16.00–22.00, and 6.18 MHz from 04.00–07.30 and 17.00–22.00; and the Aegean islands service may be audible from 03.00–23.15 GMT on 227 MW (1323 kHz).

In the Gazimağusa and Lefkoşa areas the signal from the British Forces Broadcasting Service in the Sovereign Bases in the south is strong. Programmes are broadcast for 24 hours a day on two channels: Channel 1 on 99.6 MHz (Gazimağusa) and 89.7 MHz (Lefkoşa); Channel 2 on 95.3 MHz (Gazimağusa) and 91.9 MHz (Lefkoşa).

Local television (BRT), transmitted to Girne from Mt Selvili and to Gazimağusa from Sinan Dağ, is on the air for roughly three hours a day on weekdays only. However, North Cypriot viewers can tune into Turkish television throughout the day and even see the news in English (though with a Turkish slant) at 22.30 on Channel 1 in summer. Dubbed British and American films are often shown with the English soundtrack simultaneously broadcast on radio (95.6 MHz and 92.5 MHz).

Police

The police force (*polis*) in North Cyprus keeps a considerably lower profile than the army, who have their own police force, the ASIZ. The civil police work in close conjunction with the Tourist Department and visitors can expect to be treated with special tolerance and helpfulness.

It is generally accepted that North Cyprus enjoys an exceptionally low crime rate; it is thus most likely that any help a holidaymaker might require from the police would be in a traffic context. Most officers speak some English. In emergencies the police telephone numbers are: Lefkoşa, 020 71311; Girne, 081 52014; Gazimağusa 036 65310; Güzelyurt, 071 42140; Lapta 082 18512; and Lefke 078 17423. To report a fire dial 199.

Consulates

Although the TRNC is not yet recognised by most of the world, offices are maintained in Lefkoşa by representatives of several foreign nations. The British High Commissioner, or one of his staff, also attends a subsidiary office in Girne between 10.00 and 12.00 on Saturday mornings in order to assist the large number of British expatriates living in the area.

The British High Commission Consular Section is in Mehmet Akif Cadd., Lefkoşa (tel: 020 71938) and open from 07.30–13.00 Monday to Friday. (The British Council shares the building, *see p. 127*). The Australian High Commission is at the Saray Hotel (open Tuesday and Thursday, 09.00–12.30, tel: 020 77332), the American Centre on Güner Türkmen Sok. (Monday to Friday 08.00–17.00, tel: 020 72443), and the German Cultural Centre in 28 Kasım Sok. (tel: 020 75161).

Religious Services

The majority of North Cypriots are Muslims and the muezzin's call to prayer echoes from the mosques five times a day: before sunrise, at midday (or 12.30 on Fridays, the holy day), late afternoon, after sunset and at about 22.30.

Anglican services (but all denominations are welcome) are held every Sunday at St Andrew's Church, near Girne castle. As we went to press, the incumbency was vacant; for up-to-date details contact P.O. Box 171, Girne. Also in Girne, Mass is celebrated at 17.30 on the first and last Sundays of each month in the small Terra Santa Roman Catholic church, Ersin Aydın Sok. (uphill, opposite the eastern end of the Dome Hotel). The Greek Orthodox church at Dipkarpaz has Communion followed by morning prayer at 08.00 each Sunday for the Greek Cypriots who have remained living here, and at the Maronite church of Ayios Georgios, Koruçam (*see pp. 110–11*), Communion is celebrated every Sunday. On 30 November (St Andrew's Day) each year a service is held in the Apostolos Andreas monastery church on Zafer Burnu (*see pp. 155–6*).

Property purchase

Many British and German nationals have chosen to live in and around Girne: Karaman and Bellapais are particularly popular with expatriates. North Cyprus has a policy of attracting further investment by foreign residents and aims to make it easy for such people to set up homes and businesses in the Republic. Already, the expatriate population is by no means all of retirement age; many younger people have started touristic enterprises such as restaurants, craft shops, etc.

Unsurprisingly, house prices are considerably lower than in most of Europe, and the climate and lack of pollution or crime are added benefits. An additional attraction for the foreigner is the higher purchasing power of his own currency.

The procedure for buying a house is long-winded, and would-be purchasers are strongly advised to make an early visit to a well-informed estate agent. Ian Smith of Duck-worth House, Karaman, has produced some very comprehensive and helpful guidance for the Celebrity Lambousa agency. He can be contacted there at Raif Denktaş Cadd., Emek Özkan Apt. Kat 1, Girne (tel: 081 52099, fax: 081 53660). One of the many pitfalls which he will assist you to avoid is negotiating for a property with no title deeds because it was Greek-owned before 1974. Peter Kneebone's Overseas General Agents (OGA), 11 Uzun Yol, Gönyeli (tel: 020 31964), can also offer invaluable help to British visitors and residents with services ranging from interpreting and assistance with land purchase, residence formalities etc. to car hire, chauffeuring and even baby-sitting.

Mercifully, there are no timeshare developments nor property touts operating in North Cyprus.

Useful phrases

yes   *evet*
no   *hayır (yok)*
please   *lütfen*
thank you   *teşekkur edirim*
hello   *merhaba*
how are you?   *nasilsiniz?*
good morning   *günaydin*
good night   *iyi akşanlar*
welcome   *hoş geldiniz*
goodbye   *allahas marladik (güle güle)*
sorry   *özürdilerim*
help!   *imdad!*

open   *açik*
closed   *kapalı*
money   *para*
how much is this?   *bu kaça?*
bill   *hesap*
left   *sol*
right   *sağ*
entry   *giriş*
exit   *çikiş*
I'd like . . .   *. . . istiyorum*
where is the hospital?   *hastahane nerededir?*
where is the post office?   *posta nerededir?*

beach   *plaj*
toilet   *tuvalet*
police station   *karakol*
pharmacy   *eczane*
postcard   *posta kartı*
stamp   *pul*
map   *harita*
tourist office   *turizm bürosu*
North Cyprus   *Kuzey Kıbrıs*
stop   *dur*
slow   *yavaş*

beer   *bira*
bread   *ekmek*
cheese   *peynir*
coffee   *kahve*
fish   *balık*
fruit juice   *meyve suyu*
ice cream   *dondurma*
milk   *süt*
tea   *çay*
water   *su*
wine   *şarap*

1	*bir*	7	*yedi*
2	*iki*	8	*sekiz*
3	*üç*	9	*dokuz*
4	*dört*	10	*on*
5	*beş*	100	*yüz*
6	*altı*	1000	*bin*

GEOLOGY AND CLIMATE

Geology

Cyprus assumed its present outline only one million years ago. Until the Pleistocene period, coinciding with the most recent Ice Age and the dawn of man, the Beşparmak and Troodos mountains stood as islands separated by a channel, the Athalas sea, which flowed over what is today the Mesarya (Mesaoria) plain. The third largest island in the Mediterranean, Cyprus lies 40 miles (64 km) south of Turkey and 60 miles (96 km) west of Syria; its total area is 3571 sq. miles (9250 sq. km) and that of North Cyprus slightly more than one third of the whole.

The north conveniently divides into three physical regions: the coastal plains, the Beşparmak mountains and the interior (Mesarya) plain.

Inland from Güzelyurt Bay the plain is watered by numerous streams which originate in the Troodos mountains to the south. Accordingly, the region is moist for much of the year and lends itself to agriculture. Sandy beaches line the shore and there are no cliffs until the coastline curves to the west near the ruins of Soli.

The narrow coastal strip extending west from Girne and as far east as Tatlisu is fertile and well populated. Lowish cliffs of clay and granular limestone line the indented shore which is punctuated by small rocky bays and sandy beaches. Towards Cape Koruçam the mountains meet the sea, their last outpost being a pudding-shaped promontory at the end of a small beach 2½ miles (4 km) west of Kayalar. The cape itself is a low-lying plateau honeycombed with small rock pools; an islet lies offshore across a narrow, shallow channel. Small pieces of pumice can be found in this corner of Cyprus, originating from the eruption of the Aegean volcano of Santorini in *c.* 1500 BC.

East of Girne, and extending to the Kirpaşa peninsula, is a series of golden sand beaches enclosed by clay and sandstone cliffs capped with limestone. At 'Lara Beach' erosion has hollowed out strange pot-holes in the sandstone; gigantic ribs of the same smooth rock lie at the foot of the beach, resembling petrified tree trunks or beached whales. Some 12 miles (19 km) east of Girne is the north coast's longest sandy beach, backed by high dunes which march inland and threaten to engulf the road. Its western end is dominated by a rock pinnacle – sandstone crowned by limestone, deceptively like a ruined castle. More of these 'towers' top similar promontories further to the east. South of the spine of hills on the Kirpaşa peninsula lies a string of sandy beaches, all difficult of access.

The knife-sharp Beşparmak (Pentadaktylos) range takes its name from a fist-like peak soaring to 2,429 ft (740 m): both Turkish and Greek names mean 'Five Fingers'. Its highest point is Mt Selvili (Kyparissovouno) (3,355 ft, 1,023 m) just south of Lapta. The ridge extends in an almost unbroken arc from Sadrazamköy in the west to Yedikonuk in the east, whence a lower spine of broken hills continues to Cape Zafer and its islands (the Klidhes) to re-emerge in south-east Turkey as the Amanus Mountains. Entirely made of limestone and marble, both faces are very steep and the southern side almost perpendicular. Water erosion has produced pinnacles, ravines and caves; the spectacular two-dimensional outline of the Beşparmak range evokes an operatic backdrop, enhanced by the fairy tale castles perched on its crags.

Last of the three geological regions, the Mesarya plain extends right across the island from Güzelyurt, through Lefkoşa, to Gazimağusa. Its northern boundary is the Beşparmak range which affects it climatically, claiming most of the rain brought on the northerly winds. Once submerged, and separating the two island ranges, Beşparmak and Troodos, the Mesarya is an extensive alluvial area, essentially flat and potentially fertile. How-

Mt Beşparmak rears like a clenched fist over the plain

Limestone pavements near Kaplıca

ever, a dearth of rain produces semi-desert conditions for much of the year. Between the plain and the Beşparmak mountains is an area of schist, forming conical hills rather lunar in their bareness. Isolated conical hills are also visible towards the southern fringe of the plain.

Climate

Latitude 35°N passes through the island just south of Gazimağusa; northern Cyprus is therefore on the same latitude as southern Crete. Its climate is basically 'Mediterranean': hot dry summers and mild winters during which almost all the annual rainfall occurs. As on all islands, the land temperatures in coastal areas are modified by the influence of the sea, being cooler in summer and milder in winter. The sea temperature itself never falls below 16°C (January and February); in August it can rise to 28°C.

Spring and autumn are short and are typified by changeable weather; heavy storms may batter the coast in spring and a westerly wind, locally known as the *meltem*, carries the influence of Atlantic depressions to this far eastern end of the Mediterranean. Notwithstanding, an average of only four wet days in April and 9.5 hours of sunshine per day demonstrates the attraction of the island in spring. Daytime temperatures in excess of 20°C in February and 26°C in April have been recorded in Girne. Sunshine hours in October are comparable to April, but the afternoons are shortened by the clocks going back at the end of September.

Summer in North Cyprus is almost completely reliable.

From mid-May to mid-September the sun shines for almost twice as many hours as in London: a daily average of around 11 hours. Humidity is low (40–60 per cent) and the high temperatures are therefore easier to bear than might be expected. These can reach 40°C on the Mesarya plain but are lower on the coasts, although skies are normally cloudless there too. Breezes are light and variable, the north-westerly *poyraz* being the prevailing wind. Its long sea track often produces hazy conditions. Convection currents can cause minor whirlwinds on the central plain; it is also susceptible to the hot, dry, dust-laden *sirocco* wind blowing from Africa.

Throughout the winter intermittent, and short-lived, stormy conditions result from fairly frequent small depressions; 60 per cent of North Cyprus' rain falls between December and February. The Beşparmak mountains have a major effect on the rainfall distribution. Clouds breaking upon the ridge water the northern slopes with around 550 mm. of rain per year, whereas in the lee of the range the Mesarya plain receives substantially less (300–400 mm.). Statistics show a worrying decline in rainfall over the last three decades and summer water shortages occur with regularity, especially in the Gazimağusa area.

Frost and snow are almost unknown in northern Cyprus, although night temperatures on the plain can dip low in winter and in February 1992 the first snowfalls for forty years blanketed the mountains above Girne.

Average Temperature Table

Month	Daytime temp. range (°C)	Sunshine (hours)	Rainy days	Sea temp. (°C)
Jan	14°–18°	169	12	16°
Feb	14°–19°	197	8	17°
Mar	15°–21°	255	7	17°
Apr	18°–23°	285	4	19°
May	21°–27°	355	4	21°
June	24°–30°	379	1	24°
July	29°–36°	399	0	26°
August	25°–36°	358	0	28°
Sept	25°–32°	321	1	27°
Oct	23°–28°	277	3	25°
Nov	18°–24°	231	6	22°
Dec	13°–17°	175	11	19°

Source: Meteorological Dept of the TRNC

NATURAL HISTORY

Flowering Plants

A heady mixture of European, Middle Eastern, typically Mediterranean and exclusively Cypriot plants make up the 1,800 species said to be found on the island. The growing season begins in the autumn as soon as the first rain has refreshed the ground. In an astonishingly short time, the dormant bulbs and seeds are awakened and the island is clothed in green.

During late September the small mauve autumn squill (*Scilla autumnalis*) pushes its way through dry stony ground, to be followed, after rain, by the white *Narcissus serotinus* and autumn crocuses. One of these (*Crocus veneris*) is endemic to Cyprus: its white flowers adorn the northern slopes of the Beşparmak range. (Resembling a crocus, but not appearing until December, is the purple *Romulea bulbocodium* which prefers sand or turf.) November brings grape hyacinths, small hyacinths (*Hyacinthella millingenii*) and the first cyclamens into bloom. The latter are quite common in a variety of shady locations, but one particular plant (*Cyclamen cyprium*) grows only in Cyprus. Its fragrant flowers are white with purple blotches at the base. A cousin, *Cyclamen persicum*, with pale pink, dark pink or white flowers, follows in December and continues until May. This is the wild parent of the cyclamen we buy as a pot plant. In the depths of winter the bright yellow and very invasive Cape sorrel (*Oxalis pes-caprae*) lights up huge areas of agricultural land, olive, citrus and carob orchards as well as roadside verges. It flowers until May, sharing its environment with wild gladioli, tassel hyacinth, anchusa and the more golden crown daisy (*Chrysanthemum coronarium*).

Anyone who has read anything on the flora of Cyprus will long to see the crown anemone. *Anemone coronaria*, in its normal and dwarf forms, may be red, pink, purple, blue or white; it grows mainly on the northern slopes of the Beşparmak mountains but there are also patches at lower level around Güzelyurt and on the Mesarya plain. Lawrence Durrell sat among them at Arapköy: 'the field appeared at first sight to be populated by a million butterflies.' Flowering may begin in December but the best displays are in early March. Sometimes mistaken for an anemone is the turban buttercup (*Ranunculus asiaticus*), whose habitat and blooming period is similar. It can be red, orange, pink, yellow or white and has less feathery leaves.

Narcissus tazetta, the polyanthus narcissus, was probably the Biblical 'rose of Sharon' as it proliferates around Damascus. Also widespread in Cyprus, it bears up to a dozen fragrant flowers on one stem. In barren places throughout North Cyprus, the miniature iris *Gynandiris sisyrinchium* thrusts its blue-purple flowers from a rosette of narrow leaves. The length of the stem increases with the altitude and new flowers appear each day. *Tulipa cypria*, a small scarlet tulip appearing to be black in full sunlight, is a true native and grows in great numbers in cornfields, especially between Çamlıbel and Lefkoşa. Other spring-flowering bulbs include the magenta field gladiolus.

More than twenty species of orchid occur in North Cyprus, including the yellow bee orchid (*Ophrys lutea*), woodcock orchid (*Ophrys scolopax*), ploughshare orchid (*Serapias vomeracea*) and a Cypriot variant of the Anatolian orchid. These all flower in March or April.

Early summer brings the asphodels which, although often found on waste ground, are said to grow only where man has once disturbed the land (and are therefore a valuable clue for archaeologists). Rock roses adorn the St Hilarion and Kantara areas, the most showy being the vivid magenta *Cistus creticus tauricus*. Yellow alyssum and pink arabis clothe the rocks and screes. In May wild paeonies may be found in the forests of the Beşparmak mountains.

Giant fennel, *Ferula communis*, is a feature of the Salamis ruins and the area around Koruçam and lines the roadside from Gazimağusa all the way to Kantara and beyond; it can reach 13 feet (4 m) in height and has branches like a tree. Greek mythology had it that it was in the stalk of this plant, which they called *narthex*, that Prometheus brought fire down from heaven as a gift to men. The borage family, all with glorious blue flowers, is well represented by dyer's alkanet, viper's bugloss and the tall anchusa.

As summer advances and the land becomes parched, thistles provide much of the colour, notably the low-growing sapphire blue *Eryngium amethystinum*, especially fine in the Iskele area. Many beaches, particularly in the east, have notable displays of the white sea daffodil (*Pancratium maritimum*), locally known as the Famagusta lily, and sea lavender or statice (*Limonium sinuatum*), a well known everlasting flower. Behind the shoreline and on open waste ground anywhere, the tall white sea squill, *Urginea maritima*, issues from its unmistakable huge bulb.

The serious botanist will be richly rewarded by a visit to

the North Cyprus Herbarium at Alevkaya (*see p. 93*). This collection of 800 plant specimens, pressed or preserved in a dilute mixture of alcohol, glycerol and formaldehyde, is the work of Dr Deryck Viney of Karaman. He has made a line drawing of each of the collected specimens, which include twenty North Cyprus endemics (seventeen of them restricted to the Beşparmak mountains), and has listed 300 more. A truly excellent enterprise, the herbarium was opened in November 1989 under the auspices of the Forestry Department in Lefkoşa and the public may visit it daily between 08.00 and 16.00. An explanatory booklet was published by the Public Information Office of the TRNC in 1991.

As a field guide *Flowers of the Mediterranean*, by Oleg Polunin and Anthony Huxley, is recommended; also the beautifully photographed *Flowers of Northern Cyprus* by Sonia Halliday and Laura Lushington, available on the island.

Trees and Shrubs

Cyprus, like most Mediterranean islands, was thickly forested until 2000 years ago. The Phoenicians and other seafarers were attracted to the island by its abundant supplies of timber, and as recently as the last century we find British consular officials complaining of the wastefulness of the islanders who would fell entire trees in pursuit of a single plank and burn the rest. As well as the piecemeal felling of trees for human use, many woodland areas were burned to clear land for grazing animals, which in turn perpetuated these clearances. The removal of tree cover from the Mesarya plain certainly contributed to the aridity that is so evident today.

However, many areas of forest remain along the ridge of the Beşparmak mountains and down the northern slopes of the range. There is great awareness of the importance of the surviving forests and these are carefully managed by the Forestry Department of the Ministry of Agriculture and Natural Resources. This body has strict control over cutting timber, replanting, designating conservation areas, maintaining forest roads and fighting forest fires.

Many different trees grow in these forests: Aleppo pine (*Pinus halepensis*), black pine (*Pinus negra*), plane, alder, funeral cypress, strawberry tree, large terebinth (*Pistacia atlantica*) and lentisk (*Pistacia lentiscus*). Endemic to Cyprus are the golden oak (*Quercus alnifolia*) and a type of cedar (*Cedrus brevifolius*). On the Kirpaşa peninsula and along the northern shore, olive and carob trees flourish; some of these are wild, but many have been planted for their fruit. Similarly, the Güzelyurt region is green with citrus plantations.

The southern side of the Kirpaşa and the Gazimağusa area are no longer well endowed with trees, although around Salamis eucalyptus and acacia were introduced by the British in an effort to hold down the sand. Stream beds are clearly discernible by concentrations of tamarisk and oleander.

Below the tree line is the *maquis*, known on Cyprus as *phrygana* but occurring all round the Mediterranean and typified by evergreen bushes, many of which are aromatic. The conspicuous red bark of the arbutus tree (*Arbutus andrachne*) makes a striking contrast to the ambient greenness. In spring, delicate pink and white cistus flowers mingle with brilliant yellow broom and purple sage.

Birds

Around 100 million birds of up to 250 species pass through Cyprus in spring and autumn, flying between Europe and the Nile delta. Many use the island as a 'refuelling stop' and others spend the winter there.

The Beşparmak range is attractive to birds of prey but all of these have become rare as a result of massive hunting and contamination by poisoned carrion. Most common among these raptors is the kestrel. Eleanora's falcon is a migrant still nesting in these mountains; legend has it that its name derives from Eleanor of Aragon, the formidable queen of the Lusignan sovereign Pierre I, who ruled Cyprus in the 14th century. The scarce breeding birds of prey include the griffon vulture (fairly common ten years ago), peregrine and Bonelli's eagle; the black kite, marsh harrier, common buzzard, hobby and red-footed falcon are passage migrants. At present none of these has been declared a protected species and they continue to be sold as stuffed souvenirs. The heights provide nesting sites for the rock dove, wood pigeon, hoopoe, crag martin, jackdaw, raven and Cretzschmar's bunting. Walkers on the footpaths along the north face of the range may be rewarded with sightings of any one of the island's seven endemic species: the Cyprus warbler, pied wheatear, Scops owl, coal tit, short-toed treecreeper, jay and crossbill.

The wetlands of North Cyprus have diminished during the present century, drained either for agriculture or as a precaution against recurring malaria. Nowadays the bird life suited to this habitat is confined to reservoirs except when prolonged rainfall floods the former marshland.

Naturally wet areas exist at Glapsides (north of Gazimağusa), in the hinterland of Güzelyurt Bay and to the south-west of Mehmetçik on the Kirpaşa peninsula. Gönyeli Reservoir on the northern perimeter of Lefkoşa is one of the island's most important bird-watching sites: around 4,000 birds were observed there on one day in December 1989. Many varieties of duck, grebe, goose and heron congregate here; also egrets, sandpipers, storks, the glossy ibis, black-winged stilt and black-tailed godwit. The water draws the mountain and lowland birds too: bee-eater, roller, stonechat, little owl and red-footed falcon all visit Gönyeli. (It is probably advisable to avoid weekends when bird-watching, as the reservoir is used as a recreation area.)

Many thousands of birds visit or inhabit the sparsely populated Kirpaşa peninsula. In spring and early summer, the foothills below Kantara host alpine swift, spectacled warbler, black-headed bunting and blue rock thrush. Multi-coloured bee-eaters gather on telegraph wires, ready to dart and glide after flying insects. The hooded crow and magpie are ubiquitous and the handsome roller perches on wires or posts watching for lizards and beetles. East of Dipkarpaz is the haunt of the threatened black francolin, still hunted along with the chukar, a rock partridge. Off Zafer Burnu, the nine small islands are the breeding site of the shag, peregrine and Audouin's gull: seabirds also haunt the cliffs around Kayalar.

North Cyprus is the home of many small songbirds including the indigenous Cyprus warbler which resembles the Sardinian warbler but has no red eye-ring. Despite the increasing efforts of pressure groups such as the KKKKD (North Cyprus Society for the Protection of Birds), many small birds continue to be trapped and netted, particularly in the remoter areas. It remains legal to shoot thrushes during the months of January and February and these appear as 'delicacies' on the winter menus of certain restaurants.

Heinzel, Fitter and Parslow, *The Birds of Britain and Europe with North Africa and the Middle East*, is recommended as a field guide.

Animals

Until 2000 BC such mammals as the pygmy elephant, pygmy hippopotamus and wild boar dominated the Cypriot scene. The sole survivor of the animal kingdom of those days is the Cyprus moufflon (*Ovis musimon*), but it is now doubtful whether this forest-loving sheep still occurs in the north. Most frequently seen these days are the fox, Cyprian hare and rabbit, long-eared hedgehog, Cyprian shrew and six species of bat.

Dolphins are scarce but occasionally swim south from Turkey.

Butterflies and Other Insects

The plethora of flowering plants supports a large and varied population of butterflies. Almost fifty species occur on the island, a few of these being endemic to Cyprus; others pass through as migrants between Africa, southern Europe and the Middle East. Springtime is the best season for observation as many are breeding then, but the warm climate ensures that some species, notably the red admiral (*Vanessa atalanta*) and the Cyprus meadow brown (*Maniola cypricola*) are in evidence throughout the year.

On first sight, many butterflies appear familiar, but they are likely to be variants on western European species: the southern white admiral (*Limenitis reducta*), for example, has a single row of black spots whereas the white admiral has a double row. Similarly, the indigenous swallowtail (*Papilio machaon giganteus*) is larger and brighter than the definitive insect. Its cousin, the scarce swallowtail (*Iphiclides podalirius*) is pale with elongated 'tails' on its lower wings. Among the more exotic butterflies are the eastern festoon (*Allancastria cerisyi cypria*), with its delicately scalloped margins, the large orange and yellow cleopatra (*Gonopteryx cleopatra taurica*) and the two-tailed pasha (*Charaxes jasius*) from Africa whose bright green caterpillars feed on the strawberry tree. David Carter's *Butterflies* is excellent for identification purposes.

The flower borders of hotel gardens are great attractors of the hummingbird hawk moth (*Macroglossum stellatarum*), a delightful insect which hovers like a hummingbird while probing for nectar with its long proboscis. Oleander hawk moths are less common, but easily recognisable by their large size and green, fawn and purple wings. A third conspicuous moth, often mistaken for a butterfly, is the golden tiger. Its body is orange with black stripes, its upper wings speckled brown and white while the lower wings are brilliant orange with dark grey spots.

Other less appealing insects find the island's climate to their taste. Mosquitoes can be a nuisance and it is well worth investing in an electric mosquito killer: a plastic device which, when loaded with a pellet and plugged into the mains, ensures overnight protection from bites. These are obtainable in pharmacies and ironmongers' shops, both in the UK and in Cyprus, the NB 40 model being compatible with the Cypriot power point. Since dining out of doors is the norm in summer and autumn, an insect repellent worn on the wrists and ankles is also very sensible.

The scoliid wasp, a black and yellow flying insect up to $1\frac{1}{2}$ inches (4 cm) long can be alarming, but is in fact not aggressive. There are three kinds of bee: honey, bumble and the large black carpenter bee found in woodland. Crickets and cicadas are usually heard rather than seen; the Cypriot grasshopper is distinctive, with an orange rump. Scorpions and spiders are not strictly insects: the former, small scaly creatures with pincers, are not common but live under stones and can deliver a painful sting; the latter may be large but are quite harmless.

Reptiles and Amphibians

Snakes are in evidence during spring and early summer, are comatose in the heat of high summer and spend the winter in hibernation. Without exception, they are frightened of human beings and only attack to defend themselves. Most snakes in Cyprus are non-venomous. Of these, the Balkan whip snake (*Coluber gemonensis*) can be up to 39 inches (1 m) long, and is yellowish-brown speckled with black; a fast mover, it catches lizards and birds on stony terrain. The large whip snake (*Coluber jugularis jugularis*) has a black back with cream underparts and, at 6 ft 6 in (2 m) when fully grown, is the longest European snake. It is able to climb trees. Ravergier's whip snake is more khaki-coloured, with darker diamond shapes along its back. Poisonous varieties include the Montpelier snake (*Malpolon monspessulanus*), which rivals the whip snake in length and also feeds on lizards; it may lurk among ruins and its bite can cause painful swellings and a headache. As elsewhere in Europe, the viper is dangerous; the Cypriot variety is the blunt-nosed viper (*Vipera lebetina lebetina*). A fat snake, it can vary in colour but the end of its tail is always yellow and horn-like. Its bite is highly poisonous and the victim should seek immediate help (*see p. 29*).

No visitor to Cyprus' ruins could be unaware of the lizards. The starred agama (*Agama stellio*) is the Mediterranean equivalent of the American iguana: very shy, it gallops rather than scuttles away when disturbed, on muscular forelegs. It can be up to 12 inches (30 cm) long, and is characterised by its raised head and alert expression. The chameleon is more likely to be seen in bushes or gardens: its colour is basically green but can change rapidly to match its surroundings. Its head is large, its tail prehensile and it has a frill around its neck.

The loggerhead turtle still comes ashore in North Cyprus to lay its eggs on remote sandy beaches; it has recently been afforded some protection during the breeding season. However, man is not its only enemy: the fox and crow populations are on the increase and both the eggs and the hatch are hunted by these predators. Land tortoises are not common.

In winter the green toad, marsh frog and Savignyi's tree frog frequent the wetter areas.

Fish

The eastern Mediterranean is considerably less well-endowed with fish than the western sector. This is attributed to two factors: Atlantic currents, the main providers of nutrients, are lost or dissipated before reaching Cyprus and, secondly, the waters of the Nile no longer enrich the sea as they did before the construction of the Aswan dam. However, almost two hundred different species live in the waters around the island – which are exceptionally clear due to a low incidence of plankton and very little man-made pollution.

Enormous sharks and rays patrol the deep waters way offshore, but are rarely seen. It is exciting to spot a shoal of flying fish (*Cheilopogon heterurus*) leaping and gliding above the water, but they never venture too near the shore. Fishermen concentrate on red and grey mullet, sea bream, octopus, sole and squid.

Inshore snorkellers can enjoy watching a host of colourful small fish which dart about in shallower water; sea urchins and sea anemones cling to the rocks. The intertidal zone is only 11–15 inches (30–40 cm) wide: this is the habitat of sea slugs, other small molluscs and of the small burrowing crabs whose holes are visible on many of the beaches.

HISTORY, ECONOMY AND INDUSTRY

Down the centuries, the geographical position of Cyprus has been the overwhelming influence on the island's history. As a frontier state on the borders of East and West, Europe, Asia and Africa, Christendom and Islam, she has been the contested prize of empire-builders and military tacticians, and a melting-pot of cultures touched by every civilization which has ever sought to extend its influence in the Mediterranean. The result has been a colourful, if turbulent, history, marked by periods of great wealth and glory, interspersed with long years of oppression and neglect. Her natural resources (timber and, above all, copper) lent her still more value in the eyes of predators, and Cyprus entered millennia ago upon the historical role she has played ever since – as a strategic pawn and bone of contention between rival powers anxious to expand or secure their interests in the eastern Mediterranean.

Neolithic Settlers

Cyprus' first settlers came from the areas in the immediate neighbourhood, areas from which her green landscape was clearly visible across the sea. For four thousand years from *c.* 7000/6500 BC (the earliest date for which there is definite evidence of human habitation on the island), settlers arrived from southern Turkey and the coastal regions of Syria and Palestine, and these people became the earliest population of the island, the 'Eteocypriots'. In the north their settlements included Kastros on the tip of Zafer Burnu (Cape Apostolos Andreas), Troulli to the east of Girne, Alsancak, Vrysin (near Çatalköy), Ambelikou (Bağlıköy) near Lefke, and Alonia (Mevlevi, Greek Kyra) and Drakos (Serhadköy, Greek Philia) in the Güzelyurt area. These Neolithic settlers lived in circular huts of stone and mudbrick (*tholoi*), enclosed within massive walls; they farmed, fished and hunted, using tools of flint and bone, buried their dead in shallow pits and made simple stone bowls and figurines. Pottery does not seem to have been introduced until about 4500 BC (later than elsewhere in the eastern Mediterranean), but with the arrival of further (Chalcolithic) settlers it developed rapidly. These later settlers also discovered a crucial natural resource on the island, copper.

The Bronze Age

The coming of the Bronze Age *c.* 2500 BC and the development of seafaring placed Cyprus firmly at the crossroads of international trade routes. Led by a new wave of Anatolian immigrants, the Bronze Age civilization of the island was a period of increasing prosperity. Trading and cultural contacts with Syria, Asia Minor and Egypt were established and, by the 14th century BC, with Mycenaean Greece. Evidence of this comes from the necropolis at Vounous, near Bellapais (which may have been a major religious centre), and pottery from Syria begins to appear as the Bronze Age culture spread. The well irrigated valleys of the Beşparmak range were the most thickly populated, but the increasing importance of mining and smelting also encouraged the development of Ambelikou near Lefke, always the area of the island richest in copper: tin for the manufacture of bronze was probably imported from Mesopotamia or Asia Minor. Horses had been introduced from Anatolia, as excavations of a tomb at Lapta have shown; also, tools and weapons imported from Crete have been excavated, and glazed beads from Egypt.

COPPER MINES

The exploitation of the copper mines brought greater prosperity to Cyprus, and in the Middle Bronze Age Lapithos (Lapta), which was probably the main copper-exporting port, became the most important population centre in the north. Life was no longer as peaceful, however: enmity arose between the eastern and western parts of the island, and the thick walls still standing at Pınarbaşı (Krini), for example, to the south of the Beşparmak range, testify to the need of individual communities to protect themselves from attacks by their neighbours. The northern edge of the Mesarya (Mesaoria) plain now became more populated, with settlements being founded at Değirmenlik (Kythrea), Ulukışla (Marathavouno), Sütlüce (Psilatos) and Boğaziçi (Lapathos); Dipkarpaz (Rizokarpaso) and Kaleburnu (Galinporni) on the Kirpaşa peninsula were also founded during this period, while Çayönü (Kalopsidha) became the chief city of east Cyprus as Lapta was of the west. At Nitovikla on the Kirpaşa, on a cliff south of Kuruova, a formidable fortress was built in *c.* 1700 BC. Tombs excavated at Lapta display considerable wealth, while Middle Cypriot pottery has been found at such places as Megiddo and Ras Shamra in Syria and Cyprus is mentioned (as 'Alashiya' or 'Asy') in Near Eastern and Egyptian tablets from the 18th century BC onwards as a copper-producing country.

The Late Cypriot era (*c.* 1650–1050 BC) saw a decline in the importance of Lapta and Çayönü as the great new city of Enkomi developed into a major trading and industrial centre. Internal dissension also declined and a degree of cultural uniformity was achieved as communications improved and powerful neighbours such as the Hittites, Ugaritans and Egyptians became more of a threat. Besides Enkomi, settlements at Güzelyurt and Paleokastro, on the coast near Akdeniz (Ayia Irini), smelted and exported copper, becoming important commercial centres. The earliest written records now appear, in a script similar to the Cretan Linear A which has been termed Cypro-Minoan and has not yet been deciphered. Correspondence between the king of Alashiya and the Pharaoh Akhenaten of Egypt suggests that in the 14th century BC the island had a single ruler and was an ally of Egypt; a generation or two later Hittite tablets refer to the island as part of their empire, but this may be mere boasting.

GREEK IMMIGRATION

From *c.* 1400 BC Cypriot contacts with the Aegean became closer (a change marked by an influx of Mycenaean pottery), and when the Mycenaean empire crumbled following the incursion of the mysterious roving 'Sea Peoples' (who may also have been responsible for the

The ruins of Enkomi (Alasia): its inner harbour enabled the city to become Cyprus' chief centre for trade with the Levant

sacking of Enkomi), Greek refugees arrived in considerable numbers, bringing with them iron-working skills and the concept of the independent city-kingdom. Some of the Sea Peoples themselves may have stayed; certainly refugees from Crete and Palestine arrived to swell the native population in these years. This is a confused period about which little is certainly known. But on Cyprus it has been established that Enkomi was abandoned in the late 11th century and Salamis built around a natural harbour nearby – the legend that the city was founded by Teucer after the end of the Trojan war probably reflects the Greek immigration. A new settlement was also founded at Lapta, which regained the importance it had enjoyed during the Early Bronze Age.

The foundation of Salamis symbolized a break with the Bronze Age. By the 9th century the Eteocypriot culture had blended with the Greek, and a new element was added in the form of the Phoenicians, attracted by the island's potential as a trading post and by its plentiful supplies of timber for shipbuilding. Not long after this we find Eusebius mentioning Cyprus as one of the great trading powers, and Cypriot goods have been found in Spain, suggesting that some islanders may have accompanied the Phoenicians westward. The island now consisted of several kingdoms: those in the north included Salamis, Soli, Khytri (near Değirmenlik) and Ledroi in the Lefkoşa area. The Cypriot kings are known to have paid tribute to King Sargon II of Assyria in 707 BC, but in general the island prospered, as the 8th–7th century Royal Tombs of Salamis clearly show – indeed by the 7th century Salamis was one of the largest and most prosperous cities of the eastern Mediterranean, 'with a cosmopolitan culture combining the exuberance and wealth of the Near East with Greek undertones', as the Cypriot historian Vassos Karageorghis has put it. After the Assyrian empire's collapse (c. 612 BC), Egypt became the chief power in the region and by 570 BC the Egyptian king Amasis was the titular ruler of the island. Nevertheless Greek connections remained strong and it is during this time that the Athenian philosopher Solon is said to have visited Philokypros, King of Soli, and urged him to move his city to a healthier site. Greek religion was predominant among the people and Egyptian culture was diluted by Ionian influences.

In 545 BC the kings of Cyprus threw off Egyptian domination and submitted voluntarily to Cyrus, King of Persia. The islanders joined in the revolt of the Ionian Greeks against Persia in 499–8 BC, but were defeated after a series of sieges: Soli held out for five months and, as a punishment for its resistance, its right to mint its own coinage was withdrawn and the fortress-palace of Vouni was built to keep watch over the city. Pro-Persian kings were installed in the major cities (in North Cyprus, notably Salamis and Soli) and two centuries of domination followed, relieved only by the idealistic and ambitious King Evagoras I of Salamis (435–374 BC), who overthrew the Phoenician puppet placed on his throne by the Persians, made an alliance with Athens and tried without success to unite the Cypriot kingdoms against the oppressor. His visionary rebellion was suppressed in 381 BC. Attempts by mainland Greeks to liberate the island likewise met with little lasting success, but the continuing contact served to reinforce Cypriot identification with Greek interests, and Hellenic culture, as reflected in art, architecture, dress and religion, became ever more dominant.

The Hellenistic Period (323–58 BC)

Only with Alexander the Great's victory over the Persians in 333 BC was Cyprus finally liberated, though Alexander did not recognise the authority of the individual kings and issued a single coinage for the whole island. On his death ten years later, Cyprus was fought over by Ptolemy and Antigonus, two of his successor generals – as always her natural resources and strategic position made her a valuable prize. The kingdoms supported different sides and the island changed hands several times until in 294 BC Ptolemy I Soter finally established his authority. Thereafter Cyprus remained part of his Egyptian kingdom for 250 years, a period mainly characterised by peace and prosperity. In the face of direct rule from Alexandria the ancient kingdoms faded away. Egyptian gods, such as Isis, Osiris and Sarapis, joined the Cypriot pantheon but Greek culture remained predominant and Cyprus produced one of the pre-eminent figures of Greek philosophy in Zeno of Kition, the founder of the Stoic school, who was born on the island in 336 BC.

Cyprus in the Roman Empire (58 BC–AD 395)

In 58 BC the Romans, now the ascendant power in the Mediterranean, annexed Cyprus, an action officially justified by the (distinctly suspect) claim that Ptolemy XI, the last legitimate male descendant of the dynasty, had bequeathed the island to Rome in his will. At first a district within the province of Cilicia (at the time governed by the celebrated orator Cicero), Cyprus was briefly handed back to Alexandria, then given to Cleopatra by Antony as a love gift; after the defeat of Antony and Cleopatra at Actium (31 BC), however, the island became an imperial province under the direct control of the Emperor Augustus, finally becoming a civil province in its own right in 22 BC.

Rome's main concern in adding Cyprus to her Empire was to drain it of its wealth, and this she lost no time in achieving. Nevertheless, considerable benefits accrued to the island from Roman rule: among them the inevitable Roman road-building programme, and the construction of new harbours, aqueducts and public buildings such as the forum at Salamis and the theatre at Soli. Furthermore, as part of the Roman Empire, Cyprus enjoyed a greater degree of peace and security than ever before. The threat of piracy was removed, the taxation system overhauled and trade flourished: wine, wheat and oil were major exports, as well as metals such as iron, silver and copper – *aes cyprium*, the Latin for copper, may have taken its name from the island, though opinions on this vary and it may have been the other way about.

In north Cyprus, the major towns under the Romans (as recorded by the mathematician/geographer Ptolemy in the 2nd century AD) were Khytri (near Değirmenlik), Lapta, Soli, Carpasia (on the north coast of the Kirpaşa peninsula), Trimithus (later Tremethousha and now Erdemli) and Salamis, the last-named remaining the wealthiest and most important city on the island even though the Romans chose Paphos as the provincial capital. Despite occasional disasters (Salamis was devastated by earthquakes in 77 AD, and an outbreak of plague in 164 AD carried off many thousands), some 450 years of largely undisturbed prosperity followed.

SEEDBED OF CHRISTIANITY

The *Acts of the Apostles* makes clear that Cyprus was one of the earliest seedbeds of Christianity, unsurprisingly in view of its proximity to the Holy Land. Many Jews had settled on the island, fleeing from the unrest in Palestine, and they provided potential converts for the early Christians, who themselves fled after the martyrdom of St Stephen. St Barnabas, born of Jewish parents in Salamis, returned to his home island with St Paul in 46 AD, making many converts including Sergius Paulus, the Roman proconsul – thus Cyprus became the first country ever to be governed by a Christian. Barnabas was later martyred in Salamis, but Christianity continued to make inroads, possibly playing its part in provoking the major Jewish revolt against Rome which took place in Salamis in 116 AD; ancient sources

The gymnasium at Constantia (Salamis), reconstructed in the 4th century AD

declare that some 200,000 Gentiles were massacred in the uprising (a figure that is hard to believe, though some authorities have surmised that the population of Salamis before the revolt may have been as large as 350,000). Whatever the true casualties, the rebels were firmly suppressed by Hadrian (the future Emperor) and all Jews were then expelled from the island, giving Christianity still more scope for expansion. By 313, when the Edict of Milan permitted freedom of worship throughout the Empire, Cyprus was overwhelmingly Christian, and in 325 three Cypriot bishops, including Spiridon of Trimithus or Tremethousha (Erdemli) who was later to become the beloved patron saint of Corfu, attended the Council of Nicaea which upheld the doctrine of the Trinity and established the Nicene Creed.

Byzantine Cyprus (395–1191)

When the Roman Empire, now enfeebled and beleaguered by Goths, Vandals and Huns on its northern borders, divided in 395 AD, Cyprus naturally became part of the Eastern empire, ruled from Constantinople (Byzantium). The early part of the 4th century had seen a terrible famine in 324, and further earthquakes a few years later in which Salamis was almost entirely destroyed: the city was rebuilt and renamed Constantia in honour of the Emperor Constantius II (337–61), but it never really regained its former glory. Nevertheless, Cyprus continued to enjoy a high degree of prosperity and security for a further two centuries.

A DREAM OF ST BARNABAS

Churches and monasteries were built all over the island, and in 478 the Orthodox Church of Cyprus was granted autocephalic (independent) status by the Emperor Zeno, as a result of the miraculous discovery by Archbishop Anthemios of the tomb of St Barnabas, the location of which had been revealed to him in a dream. This providential event occurred just as the Cypriot church was about to be subordinated to the See of Antioch; but Anthemios, having dug beneath a carob tree in the place instructed by Barnabas in his dream, discovered the saint's remains together with a copy of St Matthew's Gospel in Barnabas' own hand, and was able to convince the Emperor that his Church, like Antioch's, had been founded by one of the Apostles. Zeno was so impressed by the miracle that he granted the Cypriot church privileges that it retains to this day, including the right of the Archbishop to wear a purple cloak, to carry an imperial sceptre instead of a pastoral staff and to sign documents in red ink. Archbishop Makarios signed the London Accord in 1959 in that historically privileged colour, and to this day the Orthodox Church of Cyprus enjoys an exceptional position, deferring only to the original patriarchates of Constantinople, Alexandria, Antioch and Jerusalem in seniority.

RISE OF ISLAM

By the early seventh century, however, the rapid rise of Islam threatened this comfortable stability, and Cyprus became a frontier station once again, this time as a pawn in the struggle between Christian Byzantium and the Muslim East. Saracen Arabs first invaded the island in 647; they were repulsed, but later attempts proved more successful. Cyprus was devastated, and in 688 the Emperor Justinian II was forced into an agreement with the caliphs. Cyprus was declared to be neutral territory, but both sides exacted tribute from the hard-pressed population and Arab raids continued for three hundred years, during which the island constantly changed hands, as Byzantium grew ever feebler and less able to defend her vulnerable possession. Constantia was finally abandoned, and other coastal cities, such as Carpasia and Lapithos, sank into decay as the population moved inland to escape the waves of predators from over the sea. Finally, in 965 the Emperor Nicephoros Phocas drove the last Arabs from the island, ushering in a new period of prosperity. Once again Christian art and architecture flourished, and new towns came to prominence, among them Lefkoşa, built near the site of ancient Ledroi and by the late 7th century already the island's most important city. Construction of the castles in the Beşparmak range – St Hilarion, Buffavento and Kantara – also began in this period.

In 1184, the island achieved independence, albeit in undesirable and despotic form, when Isaac Comnenos, a junior member of the imperial Byzantine family and governor of Tarsus, seized control of Cyprus and declared himself Emperor, ruling with avaricious brutality for seven years. Comnenos' usurpation was finally to sever the island's links with Byzantium, for chance dictated that his oppressive reign was to be ended by a Westerner, Richard I of England, whose intervention would inaugurate centuries of domination by Europeans.

Richard and the Templars

The Seljuk Turks under Saladin had recaptured Jerusalem in 1187 and Cyprus' geographical position placed her on the route of the Crusaders from Western Europe to the Holy Land. Isaac Comnenos, in return for Saladin's protection, had promised the Saracens to lend them no assistance; so when in 1191 the ships of Richard Coeur de Lion, on their way from Messina to join the Third Crusade, were separated by a storm and one of them ran aground off Cyprus, he had no hesitation in seizing and imprisoning the passengers. Unfortunately for him, they included Princess Berengaria of Navarre, Richard's recently acquired fiancée, and Queen Joanna of Sicily, his sister (and in fact a relative by marriage of Comnenos himself). Richard, who had found shelter on Rhodes, sailed to Cyprus to demand an explanation, defeating an unrepentant Comnenos and taking Limassol castle, where he proceeded to marry Berengaria (who was crowned Queen of England in the same ceremony). Aided by Guy de Lusignan, the deposed King of Jerusalem, Richard then hunted Comnenos down, taking Lefkoşa, the mountain castles and Girne in the process. Cyprus was now a British possession and the Lionheart redistributed lands and appointed English-style justices and sheriffs before proceeding to Acre to join the Crusade. Once there, however, a shortage of funds and troops persuaded him to sell the island on to the Knights Templar, the Order formed in the twelfth century to protect pilgrims journeying to Jerusalem after the First Crusade. But Richard's price (100,000 bezants) meant that the Knights had to impose punitive taxation levels to recoup their investment, and without sufficient forces to subjugate their unruly possession they were soon compelled to beg Richard to take the island back. Richard obliged (though without refunding their down payment), and then handed the troublesome territory to Guy de Lusignan as some compensation for the loss of his Kingdom of Jerusalem.

The Lusignans (1192–1489)

The following three centuries were to be the most brilliant in Cyprus' history. The Lusignan family originated from the French village of that name in Vienne (near Poitiers), and their influence on the island was spectacular – under successive Lusignan kings, Cyprus became celebrated worldwide for its architectural splendours, its men of letters and above all for its fabulous wealth.

When the Lusignans took possession, Cyprus was virtually destitute. But after the fall of Acre in 1291 the island was to become the most eastern bastion of Christendom and, as such, the leading market for trade in silk, leather, spices and all the exotic merchandise of the Near East. Famagusta became one of the wealthiest cities on earth, famed for its luxury, effeminacy and conspicuous expenditure – one Famagusta merchant was reputed to have given his daughter on her marriage a jewelled headdress worth more than all the regalia of the Queen of France, and Dante's *Paradiso* refers to the city as an epitome of worldliness. Most of the great buildings we see today were constructed during this period, including St Nicholas' cathedral in Gazimağusa (now the Lala Mustafa Paşa Mosque), where the Lusignan monarchs were ceremonially crowned as Kings of Jerusalem, St Sophia's Cathedral (Selimiye Mosque) in Lefkoşa (1209–28) and Bellapais Abbey (1206). In addition Girne castle was built (by Jean d'Ibelin) and the by now crumbling Byzantine castles of St Hilarion, Buffavento and Kantara were refortified.

THE GOLDEN AGE

This 'golden age', however, was essentially imposed on Cyprus by a foreign ruling class. The indigenous islanders had little share in either the wealth or the glory of Frankish Cyprus. The Lusignans had ruled Jerusalem by the feudal system and lost no time in imposing the same arrangement in Cyprus, reducing most of the inhabitants to virtual serfdom. Worse still, the Orthodox church was suppressed in favour of the Latin (Catholicism) – which after considerable dissension was formally confirmed as the official religion by the *Bulla Cypria* issued by Pope Alexander IV in

Frankish magnificence: the great west window of Famagusta cathedral

1260. The merchants and the upper class of Crusader grandees (French-speaking and, because of the Lusignans' need of a strong aristocracy to keep the disgruntled peasantry in its place, augmented with middle-ranking nobility from Europe who were allotted feudal estates) made fortunes, but the bulk of the original population was increasingly alienated.

The Lusignans' importation of foreign aristocrats produced its own problems. When Palestine was recaptured by the Mamelukes, the Knights Templar and the Knights Hospitaller withdrew to the island to swell the ranks of the upper class; substantial contingents of Genoese and Venetians, too, bitter trading rivals all over the Mediterranean at this time, settled in Cyprus, and their rivalry culminated in 1372 when a dispute over who should hold the right-hand rein of King Pierre II's horse at his coronation provoked riots of such proportions that the Genoese fleet invaded and took Famagusta, holding the city for a century.

For all the gluttony, decadence and luxurious living with which it was associated, however, the Lusignan era was undeniably spectacular, and the dynasty left a greater mark on Cyprus than any other of the island's many foreign overlords. King Hugues III, for example, was a true Renaissance man – soldier, learned scholar, founder of monasteries and kindly ruler: St Thomas Aquinas dedicated his influential *De Regimine Principum* to him. Despite a devastating plague in 1349, Hugues IV continued to rule over an increasingly prosperous kingdom, and under his successor, Pierre I (1359–69), Cyprus reached an apogee of wealth. A colourful and tragic figure (his story is recounted in Chaucer's *Monk's Tale*), Pierre tried to revive the crusading spirit, touring the courts of Europe to solicit support, and enjoying a degree of short-lived success before he was murdered by his nobles. After him, the power of the Lusignans was undermined, both by the Genoese capture of Famagusta, and, in 1426, by the invasion of the Mamelukes of Egypt, who compelled Cyprus to pay them a huge indemnity. The discovery of the Americas and the opening of new trading routes around the Cape of Good Hope also contributed to a decline in Cypriot prosperity.

In 1468 Jacques II, having seized the throne from his sister Charlotte, married a 15-year-old Venetian beauty, Caterina Cornaro, thereby securing the Serenissima's protection against the Ottoman threat. Only a year later, however, both Jacques and his infant son were dead (in suspicious circumstances, it goes without saying) and Queen Caterina ruled alone, her position maintained (as long as it suited them) by the Venetians. When Alfonso of Naples proposed marriage to Caterina, however, Venice felt compelled to react and on 26 February 1489 she was 'encouraged' to abdicate, and the banner of St Mark was unfurled over Cyprus. The long, romantic reign of the Lusignans, said to possess 'fairy blood', was at an end[1].

---

[1] Lusignan blood, doubtless, still flows in the veins of sovereigns and aristocrats all over Europe, but the last known descendant of the line is said to have been an obscure old lady, Miss Eliza de Lusignan, who died in Lower Edmonton, London, at the end of the last century after a lifetime spent as a governess.

The Venetians (1489-1571)

For the Venetians, Cyprus was first and foremost a useful trading post and strategic military outpost in the battle to contain the encroaching Muslim hordes which everywhere threatened her overseas possessions. The island's resources, wheat, sugar, salt and cotton, were exploited, and they lost no time in fortifying her cities; the mountain castles were dismantled, but Famagusta's defences were replaced with new walls incorporating massive bastions (the work of Giovanni Girolamo Sanmichele) and a remodelled citadel (Othello's Tower). In Nicosia they went even further, transforming a cultured, cosmopolitan city of gardens, churches (250 of them), palaces and 50,000 polyglot inhabitants into a military machine. Everything in an area extending for nine miles around the city's heart was demolished in the interests of a clear field of fire (a process in which numerous splendid Lusignan buildings, including the historic monastery of San Domenico with its royal tombs, were sacrificed), and between 1567 and 1570 they constructed the walls around the city which still stand, forming a perfectly symmetrical ring 3 miles in circumference.

No sooner were the walls finished, however, than the Ottomans arrived, breaching Nicosia's defences in less than six weeks and slaughtering 20,000 of the inhabitants – the population was not to reach this figure again until well into our own century. Kyrenia capitulated immediately, and Famagusta alone remained as the last outpost of Christendom in the east. Behind its immense walls the city held out for ten months, its 8,000 defenders under Marco Antonio Bragadino heroically resisting a besieging force of some 200,000. However, the hoped-for relief from Venice never arrived and the Turks dug enormous trenches around the walls, enabling them at last to fill in the defensive ditch and raise towers from which they could fire into the city – 100,000 cannonballs are said to have fallen on it, some of which can still be seen today. On 1 August 1571, Famagusta surrendered.

The Venetian commander's punishment for holding out so long was spectacularly cruel. After two weeks of torture, mutilation and humiliation Lala Mustapha (who had lost some 50,000 troops during the siege) finally had Bragadino publicly flayed outside the cathedral, after which his body was quartered and his skin stuffed with straw and paraded derisively through the city on a cow, before being shipped to Constantinople.

Venetian rule over Cyprus had lasted only 82 years and,

apart from their military architecture, left curiously few traces – perhaps only in Girne is one aware of their sojourn on the island. Their occupation was generally marked by decay; drought, epidemics, earthquakes and a plague of locusts added to the miseries of the population. Cordially disliked by the inhabitants and themselves always expecting the inevitable attack from the Turks (Cyprus seems to have been a deeply unpopular posting for Venetian officials), they never felt at home in this strange island with its peculiar mélange of races and languages, its alienated peasantry and its decadent upper class. Their rule was harsh and corrupt, with punitive levels of taxation which reduced the serfs (who formed over half the population) to penury, while trade withered as wealthier Greeks and others who had made fortunes under the Lusignans emigrated, some of them, even, to Turkey.

Ottoman Cyprus (1571–1878)

The disastrous loss of Cyprus finally provoked the European powers to concerted action, and later in 1571 the Turks were famously defeated by a combined Christian fleet at Lepanto. But for Cyprus it was too late, and the island now embarked on 300 years of Ottoman rule.

Despite the cruelty displayed in their conquest of the island, the Turks were initially welcomed by the islanders, who had little cause to love the Venetians. Enthusiasm for the new rulers increased when they dismantled the feudal system and banned the Latin church, converting all the Catholic places of worship to mosques. Greek Orthodoxy, suppressed since the end of the Byzantine era, was encouraged, the Turks soon coming to appreciate how conveniently its leadership might be used as an extension of their administration. But, like the Venetians, the Ottomans' main interest was in exploiting the island, and taxes remained heavy, causing widespread destitution; a disastrous famine further aggravated the Cypriots' lot, reducing the population, it is said, from an estimated 150,000 to 25,000 within only two years.

The Ottomans' legacy on Cyprus in respect of architecture was negligible and the centuries of their rule were chiefly marked by neglect. As late as 1862 the British vice-consul reported: 'The government derives a revenue of 230,000*l*. (from Cyprus), . . . 200,000*l*. finding its way to the treasury at Constantinople. Nothing whatever is spent on the improvements of the country, no roads are constructed, no bridges thrown across the winter torrents.' He added, however, that although the population had good reason for discontent, the Greek element had no more reason to complain than the Turkish, who under the Ottomans probably came to represent about a fifth of the population (in 1821 about 100,000). The Turks did not intermarry with their Christian neighbours, but historians of all periods agree that relations between the two elements in the population were generally amicable and both suffered equally from the avarice and exploitation of their masters, and indeed combined against them.

The administrators sent from Constantinople were usually inefficient, and frequently lazy and corrupt, and gradually the bishops took more and more control of the island's affairs. By the late 18th century they had become so powerful that the Pashas became alarmed; and, as calls for the liberation of mainland Greece grew in vehemence, they organised a purge of the senior clergy, inaugurating a reign of terror which drove many Cypriots to leave for Greece. Nevertheless reforms in 1839 brought a measure of representation to the people and on the whole, the condition of the Cypriots was probably better than that of other Christian subjects of the Ottoman Empire by the time the island underwent yet another change of administration.

The Ottoman empire at its peak extended from Austria to Egypt, but after its forced withdrawal from Vienna in 1683, it gradually contracted and sank into decline. Greece eventually gained its freedom in 1827, and in 1878 the Anglo-Turkish Convention, devised by Disraeli, leased Cyprus to Britain (for a sizeable rental) in return for British support against the belligerent Russians – the magnificently grandiloquent document from the Sublime Porte which authorised the change can be read in Sir Harry Luke's fascinating *Cyprus under the Turks*. (Britain had become aware of the strategic value of the island following her experiences in the Crimean War and the 1869 opening of the Suez Canal.)

A High Commissioner was appointed, who governed the island with an elected Legislative Council. As so often before, most of the islanders welcomed their new masters. Corruption was largely eradicated and the infrastructure and education system improved; for the first time, the Greek population were permitted to participate in the administration of their island.

British Rule (1878–1960)

When Turkey entered the First World War on the German side, Britain formally annexed Cyprus. (Ironically in view of later developments, Britain offered the island to Greece in

1915 in exchange for her entering the war on the Allied side, but Greece refused, preferring to remain neutral; had the offer been accepted *enosis* would never have become an issue on the island, with consequences for later Turkish–Greek relations about which one can only speculate.) The war ended, Atatürk's Turkey finally renounced all claims to Cyprus at the Treaty of Lausanne and on 16 August 1925 the island became a British Crown Colony and member of the Empire, with George V being represented in Lefkoşa by a governor. Turkish and Greek Cypriots alike became British citizens.

The British suppressed sporadic rioting in favour of independence (most seriously in 1931, when Government House was burnt down), and it was not until after the Second World War (in which some 30,000 Cypriots fought on the Allied side) that demands for self-determination became more pressing. A plebiscite in 1950 purporting to show (somewhat improbably, it is true) that 96 per cent of the population favoured independence was rejected by the authorities, with the result that in March 1953 EOKA (the National Organisation of Cypriot Fighters) was formed. Under the joint leadership of Archbishop Makarios III and George Grivas (who adopted the *nom de guerre* of 'Dighenis' after the legendary Byzantine hero), EOKA embarked on a guerilla campaign against the British, with independence, and ultimately integration with Greece (*enosis*), as its declared aim. In retaliation, the Turks formed their own resistance movement, the TMT. Several EOKA members were executed by the British and Makarios was briefly exiled but recalled in 1957 having, he claimed, repudiated *enosis*.

After four years of terrorism and some 500 deaths, the British bowed to the pressure and on 19 February 1959 the London Accord was signed by Britain, Greece and Turkey, as well as Archbishop Makarios for the Greeks and Dr Fazıl Küçük for the Turkish Cypriots. A new constitution was drawn up, and EOKA terrorism ceased. In December of that year Makarios and Küçük were duly elected as the first President and Vice-President respectively of the Republic of Cyprus, officially created on 19 August 1960 and admitted into the United Nations and the British Commonwealth the following month.

Dr Küçük is on record as having expressed his full confidence in the future of the Republic of Cyprus as long as Archbishop Makarios remained in office and there was no outside influence. But unfortunately the new constitution, a complicated system of checks and balances designed to protect the Turkish minority, rapidly proved unworkable.

Both the Greek president and the Turkish vice-president (representing only 20 per cent of the population) were to enjoy veto powers, and all government, police and military posts were to be proportionately allocated to the two communities; bi-communality was introduced at every level, from the government down to the law courts (where members of each community were to be tried only by their fellows) and local government (where major towns had separate authorities for each community). Importantly for the future, the London Accord also granted each of the guarantor nations (Britain, Greece and Turkey) the right to military intervention in the event of a breach of its terms.

Efforts to alter the constitution were naturally resisted by the Turks, since without the safeguards it embodied Greek domination and, it was realistically feared, an eventual declaration of *enosis* with Greece was inevitable. Almost immediately a series of disagreements broke out and in December 1963 concentrated attacks were mounted on Turkish Cypriot communities; many Turkish Cypriots were killed and the Turkish population of Lefke besieged by Greek vigilantes, while Girne was seized by Greek Cypriot police. Over a hundred Turkish villages were destroyed, producing thousands of refugees, and as the Turkish population withdrew into defensive enclaves, the British and later the UN[1] were compelled to send troops to keep the two communities apart. The so-called Green Line was drawn across Lefkoşa in December 1963, and Paphos (a third of whose inhabitants were Turkish, while many outlying villages were entirely so) was similarly divided.

Meanwhile the Turks took possession of St Hilarion, thereby gaining control of the main Lefkoşa–Girne road so that Greeks could only travel along it once a day in a UN-protected convoy. (The unexpectedly fast road between Çamlıbel and Lefkoşa was built at this time, to enable Greek commuters to reach the capital from Girne without running the gauntlet of the Turkish enclave just south of the town.)

Rumours abounded: 5,000 Greek troops were said to have been smuggled into a secret hideout in the Troodos mountains, while the Turks were alleged to have landed volunteer troops at Erenköy (Kokkina), the only Turkish

---

[1] Soldiers from Australia, Austria, Britain, Canada, Denmark, Finland, Ireland, New Zealand and Sweden were involved in the UN operation, and troops of some of these nations, wearing the blue berets of UNIFCYP, are essentially still fulfilling this role today; in addition they ensure the supply of necessary commodities to the remaining Greeks of Dipkarpaz (*see p. 154*) and maintain essential services such as water and electricity where they cross the border between the two parts of the island.

village on the north coast which enjoyed direct access to the sea. The Greeks blockaded and bombarded Erenköy and were only driven off by aerial attacks from the Turkish mainland – it took UN intervention to prevent the incident from developing into a full-scale war. Further skirmishes followed and a phoney war ensued: Turkish Cypriots were excluded from government at all levels and their enclaves subjected to economic blockade. In 1971 Grivas returned to the island and in defiance of Archbishop Makarios started EOKA-B, preying on isolated groups of Turks and even Greeks who appeared to support Makarios' more conciliatory approach. As the island drew nearer to effective partition, inter-communal talks began, but Makarios would settle for nothing less than a fully Greek state (*enosis*, now that mainland Greece was ruled by a military junta and Turkey had demonstrated its willingness to fight, was less appealing, but inevitably remained a potential option), while the Turks saw partition (*taksim*), or at least bi-zonal federation, as their only hope of security.

Cyprus today

In early 1974 Grivas died; the same year, Makarios was overwhelmingly re-elected after renouncing (or at least postponing) *enosis*, and felt secure enough to purge his administration of pro-EOKA elements and insist that troops from the Greek mainland be withdrawn from the island. This proved the catalyst: under the former EOKA terrorist Nikos Sampson, and urged on by the Colonels' regime on the mainland, Greek officers of the National Guard deposed Makarios on 15 July 1974, and Rauf Denktaş, by now the leader of the Turkish Cypriots, called on Turkey to intervene under the terms of the Treaty of Guarantee to uphold the constitution and avert the threat of *enosis* occurring by default. The Turks responded swiftly; approaches to Britain having failed to elicit any support, they landed 40,000 troops west of Girne and dropped paratroopers on St Hilarion and northern Lefkoşa.

To the Greek Cypriots this was an invasion, but to the Turks a deliverance. While British troops airlifted 11,000 tourists, service families and refugees out of Akrotiri in the biggest airborne operation since Berlin, the failure of initial talks allowed the Turks to push forward beyond Güzelyurt and up the Kirpaşa Peninsula. In Athens, the regime of the Colonels collapsed, and as a result a ceasefire was agreed for 18.00 on 16 August; just before it came into effect the Turks were able to respond to appeals from Turkish villages south of Güzelyurt, to fight their way down to Akıncılar (Louroujina), home to 1,500 Turkish Cypriots, and to secure Gazimağusa: they were, however, unwilling to occupy the undefended suburb of Maraş (Varosha), so the area remains a ghost town of overgrown villas and crumbling luxury hotels to this day. The line to which they had advanced by the time of the ceasefire became the so-called 'Attila Line' (from the Turks' name for their military operation: strictly, only the section dividing Lefkoşa is the 'Green' Line), with a UNIFCYP-patrolled buffer zone beyond which occupies some 1 per cent of the island's area and is accessible only from the south.

In December 1974, Makarios returned to lead a country that had lost about a third of its territory, including areas that had previously produced much of its wealth. In February 1975 the North formed itself into the Turkish Federal State of Cyprus with Denktaş as president, and during August of that year a wholesale 'mutual exchange' of populations took place under UN supervision, with some 120,000 Greeks being relocated in the south while 65,000 Turks moved to the safety of the north – you can still see allocation numbers roughly painted on the walls of houses in many villages in North Cyprus, which date from this operation. In general, the present rule is that Greek property may be occupied but is not owned by the new occupiers, who are not entitled to sell it on. There is still some resentment over the allocation of property, not surprisingly given the haste with which such a major dislocation had to be handled: in the country, people will tell you of cases where large houses and fertile lands were given to fellow-villagers who were known to all as the laziest and least deserving members of the community when they lived in the south.

The Turkish Republic of North Cyprus (TRNC) was formally declared on 15 November 1983, and since then negotiations between the two communities have continued without success. The Greeks want unification, but the Turks not unnaturally fear for their rights and security were the UN and Turkish troops to be withdrawn. Most of them, even if they have friends among the Greek community, want partition (*taksim*) of some sort, but *not* unification with Turkey: the mainland Turks are regarded as different, and the settlers brought in from Turkey to swell the population (estimated at some 20,000 and often ex-nomads with a fairly primitive lifestyle) arouse considerable resentment. Their problem is the economic constriction resulting from the reluctance of other nations, under pressure from the Greek Cypriots, Britain and the USA, to recognise the TRNC: so far only Turkey and (very recently) the Soviet republic of

Nakhichevan have done so. Many Cypriots on both sides will tell you that the British did a disservice to the island in leaving; and most thinking Greeks, especially in the light of recent events in Yugoslavia and Russia, accept that national integration would be a long and difficult process. An article in the Greek Cypriot paper *Philevtherios* in August 1991, for example, pointed out that the wedding of a Greek girl in Dipkarpaz to a Turk had recently incited demonstrations that came close to armed confrontation. 'If in the early years of a federal republic', asks the writer, 'a Turk from Alsancak rapes a Greek Cypriot woman or if a Greek murders a Turk in Dikmen what will happen?'

So a permanent solution to the problems of Cyprus may still be a long way off. Greek Cypriots speak for Cyprus in the UN and maintain an effective propaganda campaign which the TRNC is ill-equipped to counter. The Greek line portrays the Turks merely as a dissident minority, and Western governments at present take the view that the 'secession' of the Turkish Cypriots was unilateral and illegal, despite being well aware of the degree to which their withholding of recognition is hampering the economic development of a potentially prosperous and successful region. Turkey's aspirations to EC membership and her increasing importance to the West, however, suggest that recognition of the North can not be denied for ever.

In the meantime the visitor does well to remember, when frustrated by the ubiquitous presence of suspicious and camera-shy Turkish troops who seem to display scant appreciation of Cyprus' heritage or the historic sites they often occupy, that the genuine warmth of the welcome that the people of North Cyprus extend to tourists and their eagerness to develop their holiday industry must necessarily be tempered by their perception of the need to maintain their own security. As any Turkish Cypriot will tell you, if the presence of some 20,000 Turkish soldiers and a land full of military zones is the price that must be paid for freedom from terrorism and being able to sleep easily at night, then it is a price worth paying. The Turks of North Cyprus have been given good cause for suspicion, and to believe that the price of liberty is eternal vigilance.

Economy and industry

AGRICULTURE AND FISHING

Despite the growth of the tourist industry, agriculture is still the mainstay of the economy of North Cyprus. The alluvial Mesarya plain is fully utilised during the autumn, winter and early spring, when the (albeit minimal) rainfall produces a harvest of wheat and barley. Only a very small proportion of the plain has been irrigated; in these parts the growing season is extended, and potatoes, vegetables and watermelons are grown for home consumption and export. Two crops of potatoes mature during late winter and early spring, many being exported to the UK, where they are among our earliest 'new season' vegetables. In the wake of improved irrigation, the cultivation of watermelons for export is becoming more important.

On the lowlands of the Kirpaşa peninsula, carob trees have been grown commercially since Venetian times: large disused 16th-century carob stores can be seen at several places along the coast. These days, the pod of the tree is crushed for animal fodder rather than human consumption, and exported to the UK and elsewhere. The north-east corner is also the principal vine-growing area of North Cyprus. Sultana, wine and table grapes are grown here, the sultanas for export. Wine production is no longer a village industry, but many grapes (mainly black) are processed for blended table wines. Tobacco is another traditional crop of the Kirpaşa but its cultivation is in decline. Market gardening, with intensive use of greenhouses, is a feature of the area around the coastal road east of Esentepe: tomatoes, peppers, beans, cucumbers, courgettes and aubergines are grown very successfully here, taking advantage of underground reservoirs.

An estimated $1\frac{1}{2}$ million olive trees grow in the coastal regions of North Cyprus. The fruit is exported and processed into oil in the TRNC. Olive trees are not usually concentrated in groves, but are juxtaposed with carob and almond trees. Citrus orchards have been planted wherever the land is sufficiently watered. The natural wetlands of Güzelyurt and Lefke support the largest plantations, but trees also flourish around Lapta and Alsancak where the limestone mountains secrete a year-round supply of water. Irrigation in the Gazimağusa area has enabled small orchards to thrive there too. Oranges, tangerines, lemons and grapefruit are grown in quantities large enough not only to provide the Republic with home-grown fruit, but also to export both fruit and fruit juice overseas. In recent years a major juice-pressing and fruit-canning industry has developed, centred on Güzelyurt; but at present the future of Lefke-born Asil Nadir's Polly Peck International, responsible for this highly successful venture, is uncertain – a cause for great concern for North Cyprus where Mr Nadir's success has been an important source of employment.

Bananas, apricots, figs, cherries, apples, pears and straw-

Agriculture on a simple scale still provides the livelihood of most of the population

berries are all grown on the north-facing hillsides west of Girne; bananas also do well at Yenierenköy on the Kirpaşa.

North Cyprus is a major producer of livestock and is fully self-sufficient in meat and eggs. Small amounts of cheese, yogurt and honey are made on the island and sold in the markets. Fishing is being developed by the government as a market-orientated industry and employs men wherever there is a harbour: Girne, Gazimağusa, Kumyalı and Boğaz each have a fishing fleet.

INDUSTRY

North Cyprus is currently investing heavily in tourism and it is hoped that this source of income will grow in importance: the climate is such that it should be possible to attract holiday-makers at all times of year. Most tourists at present come from neighbouring Turkey; of those who visit from elsewhere the British are in the majority, with the Germans taking second place. A few hotels pre-date the division of Cyprus, but most are recently built and meet the high standards expected by the modern traveller. The Republic has a growing number of villa developments to cater for the trend towards independent holidays. Numbers of foreign visitors have increased steadily since the opening of Ercan airport in 1975, though a temporary drop occurred in 1990–91, when the Gulf War deterred many people from visiting the eastern Mediterranean. At present all flights from western Europe to Ercan are routed via Izmir or Istanbul and 'through' flights are only available on specific days of the week. Another international airport was opened at Geçitkale in 1986, but has so far only been used when Ercan is closed for repairs.

Drying fleeces on the Kirpaşa peninsula

Inevitably the construction industry has boomed in response to the need for tourist accommodation and improved roads.

Until 1963 Gemikonaği was a busy port, exporting copper and iron pyrites to the UK, USA, Germany and other European countries; today a ruined jetty, the hulks of cargo boats and abandoned machinery lie stranded there, reminders of the time when Cyprus was one of the world's major exporters of minerals. No mines remain in North Cyprus, but the Beşparmak mountains are quarried for lime, marble and limestone. Gypsum is exported from Kalecik, north of Boğaz, where there is also an important oil terminal.

In the remoter areas, the industry of a bygone age still lingers on: charcoal-burning can be seen near the road between Soli and Vouni, and drying fleeces hang from the balconies of houses on the Kirpaşa, their wool awaiting carding and spinning for carpet-making. A handful of clothing factories make cotton garments for export, mainly to the UK.

SPORTS AND ACTIVITIES

Sport

FOOTBALL

The game enjoys a passionate following in Cyprus; the North has 36 league teams, divided into 1st, 2nd and 3rd divisions. Matches are held on Saturdays and Sundays, the main grounds being at Lefkoşa, Girne and Gazimağusa.

GOLF

North Cyprus has as yet no official golf course, but visitors will be made extremely welcome at the CMC Golf Club at Yeşilyurt (*see p. 114 for directions*). Originally laid out by the Cyprus Mining Corporation in the 1920s, the course has only 7 holes, but members contrive to get 18 out of it; it was remodelled in 1949 by Mr Ian Cooper, a doughty 79-year-old who worked for the Corporation and still lives nearby. He has fought heroically to keep the course alive despite the events of 1974 and the subsequent presence of an army camp immediately adjacent (with which good relations are assiduously maintained). The course (which has greens only from November to March, the rest of the year they are 'browns'!) is run on a shoestring, financed by nominal green fees which cover the cost of sweeping and maintenance.

The course is open daily, but the 50-odd members (mostly British but including a few enthusiastic Cypriots) usually meet on Tuesday, Thursday and Sunday mornings, many driving 40 miles from Girne for their game. On other days Mr Cooper keeps the clubhouse open and is delighted to welcome visitors. There are a few sets of clubs available for visitors to borrow, though players are asked to bring their own if possible; also beer and sandwiches, as there is no restaurant. The atmosphere in the clubhouse is informal and welcoming and you will be proudly shown press cuttings and a letter from the Royal and Ancient congratulating Mr Cooper on his tremendous efforts to keep golf alive in North Cyprus. Anyone at all interested in the game is recommended to visit the CMC club, if only to celebrate the club's survival.

HORSE-RIDING

At the time of writing four establishments offer horse-riding. Two of these are at Karaoğlanoğlu: Tunaç Riding School (tel: 081 52855), owned and run by Mr Ziya Tunaç, has 40 horses which he hires out at the rate of c. £3.50 an hour between 06.30 and 08.00 and after 17.00. Children are given tuition at weekends. An inclusive price of £12–13 is charged for a day's riding (11.00–17.00) with a picnic lunch. Dörtnal Riding School, slightly nearer Girne, is owned by an ex-employee of Mr Tunaç: it has six horses for hire between 07.00 and 08.00 and between 16.00 and 19.00. He charges about £5 per hour, with no extra charge for an accompanied ride. There is no phone but he likes a booking to be made. Riding is also available to both residents and non-residents at the Cyprus Gardens, beside the sea 11½ miles (18½ km) north of Gazimağusa, and at the Mare Monte Hotel, 7 miles (11 km) west of Girne.

HUNTING

Shooting is immensely popular among the Cypriots and at least 3,000 adult males belong to hunting associations. Five times that number hunt independently; it is cheap and easy to obtain a licence.

There are three seasons during which the sport is legalised. The general shooting season spans the months of November and December when rabbits, chukar (partridge), snipe, woodcock and black francolin are shot (this last is of great concern to conservationists as its numbers have diminished alarmingly). The thrush shooting season follows for the next two months, during which up to a million birds, mostly overwintering song thrushes and robins, may be killed. Thirdly, the turtle-dove shooting season takes place on two days a week between late April and late May. As this period coincides with the spring migration, many other species are illegally dispatched.

Tourists may obtain a permit for the temporary importation of a sporting gun by applying to the Ministry of the Interior in Lefkoşa (tel: 020 73648). Automatic and semi-automatic firearms are prohibited, but air and shotguns are allowed within prescribed limits.

SAILING

North Cyprus would appear to be ideal for yachtsmen, but in fact there is not much sailing and the sea around the Republic is noticeably empty most of the time. It is true

The castle of St Hilarion perched on its towering crag

Church of Ayios Philon, Carpasia   (below) The Beşparmak
range from Buffavento castle   (bottom) 'Turtle Beach'

that, during high summer, lack of wind might be irksome but a more major problem is posed by the string of army camps which guard the coastline and are sensitive about the presence of independent craft. The relevant maritime chart marks the forbidden areas which include passage around the Kirpaşa peninsula.

However, yachts which arrive in Girne old harbour will find moorings, repair facilities, showers, a laundromat and sundry restaurants. Harbour dues were introduced in 1991, but these are very small; immigration formalities must be dealt with at the new (commercial) harbour. Gazimağusa has minimal facilities, including one or two chandlers.

It is probably best to hire a dinghy from Dolphin Sailing, which operates between May and October from the beach below the Denizkızı Hotel west of Girne and is a recognised RYA establishment. The resident instructors, Chris Cockshott (ex-National Dinghy Sailing coach for the RAF) and his son Alex, a senior RYA instructor, are always on hand if tuition is required.

Sailing dinghies and catamarans are also available for hire to residents of the Palm Beach and Salamis Bay hotels at Gazimağusa. Instruction is optional.

SQUASH

The TRNC's squash club is in Bahadır Sok., Lefkoşa, behind the State Theatre. It is open all the year round, from 08.00–23.00 daily. Only one court is available at present, though further building is in progress. Consequently, booking is advisable (tel: 020-74064); the charge for non-members is £1.50 per hour. The club both hires and sells squash equipment.

SWIMMING

Historically the Turkish Cypriots have little affinity with water and many of the older generation have never learned to swim. The younger people are keener, but observation shows that most bathers are holiday-makers.

The unpolluted sea, devoid of dangerous currents, is perfect for swimming and snorkelling. Colourful small fish may be seen darting through the shallows. Off most beaches in the north the water gets deep only gradually, but swimmers should always be aware that there are no lifebelts by the shore nor any lifeboat patrolling the coast.

Beaches which are fronted by hotels or restaurants may charge a small admission fee (6000 TL is typical at the time of writing), which entitles visitors to use any amenities

'Bambi beach' (Yavuz Çikarma Plaj)

provided: car park, lavatories, changing cabins, showers, umbrellas and sunbeds. If an army camp lies directly behind the beach you should not go near. Almost certainly there will be a warning notice.

Topless bathing and sunbathing are not forbidden by law, but neither is usual except at some hotel swimming pools.

Between June and mid-August, great care should be taken when digging holes for sun umbrellas on the more remote beaches, as this may disturb or destroy the nest of a loggerhead turtle.

TENNIS

Courts at some of the major hotels may be used by non-residents on payment of a fee of £2–£2.50 an hour. West of Girne, there are courts at the Mare Monte and Celebrity Hotels, the LA Holiday Centre and Jasmine Court Apartments; east of Girne at the Club Acapulco (March to November only). In the Gazimağusa area there is tennis at the Salamis Bay Hotel and the Sea View at Boğaz. All these have equipment for hire but the Celebrity offers no changing facilities. The Salamis Bay and the Sea View have floodlit courts: those at the former are open until 23.00 daily all year round. The Palm Beach and Park Hotels, in and near Gazimağusa, have tennis courts only for their guests, but there are municipal courts between the Palm Beach Hotel and La Cheminée restaurant.

In the capital, the Lefkoşa Field Club, off Mehmet Akif Cadd. and near the British High Commission, has floodlit tennis courts, changing facilities and a cafeteria. However, as this club is in a military area, non-members must obtain a permit one week in advance by telephoning Mr Ilter Sami Şanel on 020 71313.

Walking

Apart from the clearly marked military areas, the walker may pass freely through the North Cypriot countryside. There are many footpaths, forestry tracks and unmade roads, although no adequate walking map to follow. In spring and autumn the walker will not be inconvenienced by the heat; winter is also a good time for walking, but rain is

Walking in the Beşparmak mountains

more likely then. Some of the most attractive walks are between the villages on the northern flank of the Beşparmak range; the whole of the north coast is panoramically displayed below. In spring the Kırpaşa peninsula also offers endless opportunities for rambling through carpets of wild flowers to the accompaniment of birdsong or the sound of the *dillidüdük*, the traditional flute of the Turkish shepherd; the area is also resonant with the traces of past civilizations. There is no continuous coastal footpath but many beaches are accessible on foot by following dirt-tracks visible from the road.

Particularly in the mountains, walkers should always be keenly aware of the risk of starting forest fires.

Water Sports

Potentially North Cyprus is eminently suitable for organised water sports, but at present this aspect of touristic development is still in its infancy. The season extends from May to October.

Onshore breezes make windsurfing very pleasurable. Boards may be hired at the Celebrity Hotel and Bungalows, Club Acapulco, Club Kyrenia, Chateau Lambousa, the Mare Monte Hotel, Denizkızı Hotel (Dolphin Sailing), Palm Beach Hotel, Park Hotel, Salamis Bay complex, Mimoza Hotel, Cyprus Gardens and Long Beach Bungalows. The average price in summer 1991 was 30,000 TL (*c.* £3.75) for half-an-hour. Tuition is not usually offered, but Dolphin Sailing are an exception.

Water-skiing is possible at Denizkızı beach (Dolphin Sailing), Club Acapulco, Chateau Lambousa and the Mare Monte, Salamis Bay and Palm Beach hotels. Terry Cockshott, an expert powerboat driver and director of Dolphin Sailing, charges *c.* £4 per trip or £8 with tuition.

Dolphin Sailing is the only parasailing operator; a flight cost about £9 in summer 1991. The same establishment is the sole venue for speedboat trips and rocket rides in which five or six people, astride an inflatable 'rocket', are towed at speed behind a powerboat. The price for this in 1991 was *c.* £2.50 (children £2).

There is no recognised diving centre in North Cyprus.

Culture and Folklore

Cultural events in North Cyprus are few. The Cyprus Turkish State Theatre in Okullar Yolu, Lefkoşa, presents regular dramatic productions but always in Turkish. Concerts by the State Symphony Orchestra are very occasional.

On a large site opposite the Girne Gate in Lefkoşa is the Atatürk Cultural Centre, which houses a concert hall, an art gallery and a lecture theatre, together with a library holding over 50,000 books (some of them in English, French and German). The entertainments provided here are diverse: orchestral and jazz concerts, film shows, plays, seminars, etc., and are sometimes aimed at an English-speaking audience.

Girne has attracted British residents for many years and at present the expatriate population is rising and its average age decreasing. The Kyrenia Society, PO Box 280, Girne (tel: 081 52434/54055), founded in 1971, organises rambles, film shows, whist drives, lectures and art exhibitions as well as patronising cultural events, some of them sponsored by the British Council. Visitors to North Cyprus are welcome to become associate members and to use the library (open 10.00–12.00, Weds and Sat, donations of books and magazines are appreciated), which is behind the main Post Office. A Turkish–German Cultural Society, with similar aims and activities, is run from 26 Kasım Sok., 15, Lefkoşa; the emphasis here is on promoting German culture and German language courses are offered.

MUSEUMS

With regard to museums, historically minded visitors will be disappointed that most of the interesting archaeological finds of North Cyprus are displayed elsewhere: mainly in the Cyprus Museum in southern Lefkoşa or in the British Museum. Girne castle, however, houses the Shipwreck Museum (*see p. 82*), of major importance in the context of world maritime history. The Güzel Sanatlar Muzesi (Fine Arts Museum, *see p. 83*), Folk Art Museum and the Icon Museum (*p. 83*) are also worth a visit. Scholars and researchers can browse through a multitude of historical documents, including the chronicles of the British administration of Cyprus between 1878 and 1960, at the National Archive on the outskirts of Girne (Çatalköy road). The Peace and Freedom Museum (*see p. 107*) is at Karaoğlanoğlu.

In Gazimağusa the Canbulat Museum is open to the public 09.00–13.30 and 16.30–18.30 in summer. There is no museum at Salamis (though the custodian has a few eligible pieces in his hut!). Beside the Royal Tombs (*p. 144*) a small museum contains some interesting exhibits, well displayed. The church of Panayia Theotokos on the western outskirts of Iskele was opened in June 1991 as an icon museum, and St Barnabas' monastery is currently being converted to the same function. Worth visiting in Lefkoşa are the Mevlevi

Tekke Museum, the Library of Sultan Mahmoud II, the Mansion of Derviş Paşa and the Lapidary Museum (*see pp. 121, 123, 125-6*). There is also a museum in Güzelyurt, beside the monastery of Ayios Mamas.

MUSIC, DANCING AND FESTIVALS

Turkish folk music has its origins in Anatolia, where it dates from the time of the Hittites (*c*. 2000 BC). To this day, musicians play the traditional tunes on instruments similar to those in use millennia ago: at least five different stringed instruments are played with a plectrum and two others with a bow; the *zurna* is a forerunner of the oboe, the *davul* a bass drum and the *ney*, also played in ancient Egypt, resembles a flute.

On public holidays, performers in colourful national dress interpret these ancient rhythms by dancing in lines, circles and semi-circles; the dances all have names, e.g. *karşilama*, *kasıklı* and *oyunları*. Such displays can be seen in front of the Othello Tower in Gazimağusa and the castle in Girne, notably on 1 April when the tourist season begins (a party atmosphere develops and there is an open buffet) and on 20 July in celebration of the Turkish landing in 1974. The orange, watermelon and grape harvests are all celebrated with music and dancing in the villages; the dates of these holidays differ each year and take no account of tourism although any visitor is welcomed. Perhaps the most noteworthy of these spontaneous festivals occur at Güzelyurt (for oranges), Yeşilirmak (for strawberries) and Aşağı Bostancı (for watermelons).

Excursions

Tour representatives in the resort areas usually have a programme of coach or minibus trips which may include a picnic meal in the price. The same excursions can be booked by the independent traveller through such agencies as Kyrenia Holidays Ltd, 95K Hürriyet Cadd., Girne (tel: 081 52968), Vipkotur, c/o the Dome Hotel, Girne (tel: 081 53769), Celebrity Tours, 5 Cumhuriyet Cadd., Girne (tel: 081 53517/8) and Ner Turizm, c/o the Palm Beach Hotel, Gazimağusa (tel: 036 67599/62001).

Typical sightseeing tours from Girne are: Gazimağusa with a visit to the Salamis ruins and St Barnabas' monastery; Bellapais abbey, St Hilarion castle and Lefkoşa; Güzelyurt with Soli and Vouni; Buffavento castle; Kantara castle with the Kirpaşa peninsula; and a mountain barbecue in the pine forest at Alevkaya. The last three of these are likely to be made in a minibus and the visit to Buffavento requires some steep walking. Prices for a full-day excursion are usually around £20. A Turkish Cypriot meal (*mezes* and probably *kup kebab*, *see pp. 17–18*) in a restaurant by Girne harbour, with transport provided, is a popular evening excursion.

From Gazimağusa, a day in Girne is an obvious choice and this is often combined with St Hilarion and Bellapais. Soli and Vouni may not be offered, in view of the distance, but there are better chances of finding an excursion up the Kirpaşa peninsula.

Various cafés around Girne harbour offer 'full day' boat trips along a small portion of the north coast, leaving at 11.00 and costing c. £13 per head (summer 1991); there are also boat trips from the harbour at Gazimağusa, which visit Salamis, Boğaz and Kumyalı on the Kirpaşa peninsula.

It is not possible to visit south Cyprus from the TRNC.

Nightlife

North Cyprus makes no attempt to attract holidaymakers seeking wild nightspots; however, some of the large hotels have discotheques, often sited in the basement or away from the main building to avoid disturbance. In Girne the **Dome Disco** is in the hotel's annexe and open from 22.00 onwards. **Tunnel Disco**, on Ecevit Cadd. (the main Lefkoşa road), boasts 'the best music and light show in town' and is also open from 22.00, as is the **Hippodrome** at Karaoğlanoğlu. In Alsancak, the **Mare Monte Hotel** has an open air disco ('groovy music, groovy people') set well away from the bedrooms: it functions from 23.00 on Fridays, Saturdays and Sundays. Further west, at Lapta, the Celebrity complex

Almost everyone eats out at weekends, when many restaurants provide live music and dancing

offers the **Lambousa Night Club** and **Celebrity Disco**, both underground and both open from 22.00. In Gazimağusa the **Palm Beach Hotel** has a disco and nightclub in its basement (open from 22.00); there is also a disco at the **Salamis Bay Hotel**. In the heart of the walled city the **Old Town Disco** occupies part of the ruined monastery church of St Francis. Nightclub floor shows and some restaurants (*see p. 23*) may feature a belly-dancing display. In North Cyprus the custom of pinning bank notes to the clothing of a newly married couple is aped by attempts to insert money into the dancer's scanty costume.

CASINOS

A surprising number of casinos are available for gamblers, mostly offering poker, roulette, *chemin de fer*, baccarat and blackjack as well as an array of slot machines. Cypriots are not allowed to visit them: ironically enough, their patrons are mostly visitors from mainland Turkey, who themselves are not permitted to gamble at home. At the **Dome Hotel**, Girne, the casino in the annexe opens from 20.00 to 04.00; the **Grand Rock Casino**, close at hand, stays open later still. There is also gaming at the **Liman Hotel** overlooking the old harbour. The **Celebrity Casino** at the Celebrity Hotel, Lapta, is open from 21.00 to 04.00. In Gazimağusa the **Palm Beach Casino** (open 22.00–04.00) is in the basement of the hotel, next to the nightclub; at the **Salamis Bay Hotel** the casino is on the ground floor. In central Lefkoşa there is a casino at the **Saray Hotel**.

Shopping

Most shops in North Cyprus are open from 07.30 to 13.00 and 16.00 to 20.00 in summer (08.00–13.00 and 14.30–18.00 in winter). Markets are only open in the mornings. As in Turkey, much of the merchandise is excitingly oriental. Brass, copper, silver, enamel, bronze and onyx articles crowd the tourist shops; one can also find meerschaum pipes, Turkish dolls and backgammon sets fashioned from inlaid wood. Unlike on the mainland, however, prices are usually fixed and haggling is not traditional.

Pottery and ceramics, made in both Turkey and North Cyprus, are everywhere; the largest showroom is the **Ceramic Centre** (tel: 020 32302), on the left of the main Girne–Lefkoşa road as it enters Ortaköy near the capital's main hospital. For genuinely North Cypriot pottery, visit **Dizayn 74**, on the main road at Karaoğlanoğlu (tel: 081 52507/53817): everything is made on the premises at this handicrafts cooperative and special orders are taken. (You are almost sure to recognise the cruets and ashtrays, as they are in evidence at most of the Republic's hotels and restaurants, customised for each establishment.)

Girne has a good selection of gift shops, many of them in the old harbour area: **Misli** and **Bakri**, both in Kordon Boyu, are crowded with ideas. The handicraft shop in the Venetian castle tower sells pottery, old goat bells, hangings and traditional Cypriot headscarves: these have embroidered lace flowers around the edges and are called *yemeni*. At the junction of Cumhuriyet Cadd. and the road to Bellapais is a shopping parade which repays a visit. **Galerie Dündar** (15–17 Türkmen Sok. tel: 081 52092), run by an expatriate woman who has lived in Cyprus since well before 1974, sells hand-crafted copper and bronze, new and antique clothing, costume jewellery and pretty greetings cards. Next door, **Nihan's** carpet shop has *kilims* (woven carpets), *cicims* (embroidered carpets) and sheepskin rugs. Almost opposite is **Merdiven** (tel: 081 51502), Girne's bookshop, which sells some English and German books. Nine miles (14½ km) west of Girne, the **Celebrity Hotel** shop is quite well stocked with souvenirs, and a few metres up the road from Karaoğlanoğlu to Karaman is a gift shop remarkable for the whimsical placards ('with peace, love and justice, we can translate life', for example) which embellish the exterior.

The old walled town of Gazimağusa has a more Middle Eastern feel than Girne; some of the best souvenirs can be found at **Halil Sarpoğlu's** shop at 40–44 Istiklal Caddesi (tel: 036 65532). Mr Sarpoğlu, a some-time teacher of geography, has assembled an enormous range of copper and onyx ornaments, smart casual clothing, leather goods, jewellery and ceramics in his very welcoming shop. Here you will find Lefkara handiwork – self-coloured embroidered linen associated with the eponymous village in southern Cyprus but, the Turkish Cypriots insist, originating as an art in Gaziantep in southern Turkey. North Cyprus lace is also on sale here. In the same street the many jewellers include **Bazaar 2000** at no. 18 and a branch of **Altınbaş**: gold is sold by weight (the price changes daily) and so the prices of the more precious pieces are not displayed in the window. **Serdar** leather at 31 Liman Yolu offers items made at the leather factory in Sandallar (*see index*). Opposite the Sea Gate, in Liman Yolu, **Petek Pastaneleri** (1 Yeşildeniz Sok. and 18 Salamis Yolu) makes up boxes of mouth-watering sweets and Turkish delight (*lokum*), while its sister shop, **Ak Petek Ticaret** (5 Yeşildeniz Sok. tel: 036 64870), sells carpets, handmade

Pottery, onyx, lace and embroidery feature prominently in Girne's souvenir shops

Turkish ceramics, woven shoulder bags and hand-carved pipes. The **Uluçay Carpet Centre** at 22 Namık Kemal Meydanı (tel: 036 67820) has a good selection of *kilims*, ceramics, pictures, embroidery, lace and other crafts; it also sells books.

In Lefkoşa, **Cyprus Corner** (tel: 020 71187) has branches in the market and north of the Selimiye mosque and offers a selection of locally made gifts and antiques. Fashionable leather clothing can be bought at **Serdar**, 5 Mecidiye Sok., and hand-woven carpets and *kilims* at **A.S. Hiçsönmez**, 31 Osman Paşa Cadd. (tel: 020 75412). In the shopping precinct of Evkaf Işhanı on Girne Cadd. are **Altınbaş**, the jeweller (unit 1) and **El Sanatları Kooperatif** (unit 13, tel: 020 71368), which specialises in lace, Lefkara work and hand-woven table linen. On the west side of Atatürk Meydanı are the premises of **K. Rüstem**, North Cyprus' main bookshop and publisher: Turkish, English and German books may be found on the crowded shelves, also a good map of North Cyprus. Lefkoşa **market**, behind the Bedestan, is busy in the mornings; very cheap basketwork can be purchased here, among other souvenirs.

Shopping in the Republic is enjoyable: the shopkeepers are friendly, but neither grasping nor importunate. Opticians dispense spectacles quickly and cheaply and almost anything can be made to order if you ask around, from a machine part to a pair of shoes. Photographic film processing is available within 24 hours in the main towns.

You may see antiquities offered for sale in North Cyprus. If tempted to buy, remember that it is illegal to export such items: seek advice from the Ministry of Tourism in Lefkoşa (tel: 020 75051) or the Department of Antiquities and Museums (tel: 020 72916).

GIRNE (KYRENIA)

Girne (Kyrenia)

Founded in the 10th century BC by Achaean settlers, Kerynia (as the city state was originally named, after a mountain in the Peloponnese) was one of the ten kingdoms of classical Cyprus. Little is recorded about the town, however, until it was fortified under the Byzantines as a defence against the Arab raids of the 7th and succeeding centuries. The castle they built was chosen by Isaac Comnenos' family as a refuge from Richard the Lionheart (*see p. 54*), but was much enlarged by the Lusignans, who used it as a residence and refortified it so effectively that it was able to withstand a siege by the Genoese in 1374 and to deter the invading Mamelukes in 1426. The Venetians also reconstructed the castle in 1554, but despite this it fell to the Turks without a struggle less than twenty years later.

Under the Ottomans Kyrenia remained a minor port and the population dwindled, but the British liked the town; the castle they used as a prison and a police training school, but they built a quay and a harbour wall and towards the end of their occupation the little town became something of an expatriate colony. **The Dome Hotel** (opened in 1939) was very much the place to be seen in and as recently as 1974 there were some 2,500 British residents, amounting to about half the population.

Today the town is still small with scarcely 6,000 inhabitants; it huddles around its pretty horseshoe-shaped harbour like many another Mediterranean port, with the mountains behind forming a picturesque backdrop. The tall warehouses around the harbour, mostly built for the storage of carobs but now housing restaurants and bars, give the town a more Venetian air than anywhere else on the island, and the atmosphere is leisurely, peaceful and romantic. The **castle** (open daily 08.00–13.00, 14.00–17.00) is entered by a bridge across what used to be the moat. Immediately to the left is a 12th-century Byzantine church, **St George of the Castle**, which stood outside the walls until the Venetians incorporated it within the castle: its ancient columns, with Corinthian capitals, doubtless came from a still earlier basilica. Ahead stretches a ramp used for drawing artillery up to the prominent rounded tower the Venetians built overlooking the harbour: the ramp passes by the **Lusignan tower**, itself a modification of the earlier Byzantine one. Above the gatehouse can be seen the Lusignan coat of arms, while the sarcophagas of the Ottoman admiral Sadık Paşa stands nearby. The central courtyard is framed to the west by a section of the original Byzantine wall, with the remains of the Lusignan royal apartments above and a roofless Latin chapel. The wall terminated in a southern tower of which the remains are visible; a passage through it runs to the massive square bastion, reminiscent of Famagusta's, which the Venetians built at the south-west corner of the castle. The north wall, of Frankish construction with castellations and arrow slits, is largely intact and the north-east tower was also left as it was; from it steps lead to a series of rooms, also Frankish but much altered when the castle became a prison. In the two furthest of these is the **Kyrenia Shipwreck Museum**, preserving the most ancient wreck ever recovered from the sea. Some 2,300 years old, this wooden ship was carrying at least 400 amphorae from Rhodes and Samos, as well as 29 basalt millstones from Kos, when it sank in 90 feet (30 m) of water in *c.* 300 BC. The four-man crew appears to have lived largely on almonds, of which some 9,000 were found preserved in jars in the hull. The ship, 47 feet (14.3 m) long and constructed of Aleppo pine sheathed in lead, was salvaged in 1968–9 by a team from the University of Pennsylvania and is carefully preserved in the castle, together with a full-size replica and other exhibits.

Dominated by the castle, the traffic-free harbour area is

The preserved timbers of the 'Kyrenia ship'; carbon dating reveals that the vessel was already at least 80 years old when it sank

the chief magnet for visitors: an idyllic spot for a stroll, a drink or a meal at one of the numerous cafés and restaurants as the shadows lengthen on the mellow stone of the old buildings and swallows wheel and scream above the calm waters. The **Folk Art Museum** here, in a converted granary, is a reconstruction of a typical Cypriot house, displaying tools, needlework and carved furniture. Behind the harbour the back streets are narrow and fairly scruffy, but there are always unexpected glimpses of the mountains peering dramatically into the town. Above the western end of the harbour rises the square pierced tower of the Archangelos church, now the **Icon Museum:** it preserves the original iconostasis of richly carved dark wood with 11 large paintings and 30 smaller panels, and icons of various periods cover the walls. Annoyingly, however, although the subjects of the icons are identified, there is no indication of their provenance. Nearby, in Canbulat Sok., some rock-cut tombs are visible, dating from *c.* 400 AD; further up the street is Girne's covered market and a tower which was once a part of the town's walls. Another relic of ancient Kyrenia is a Greco–Roman tomb at the end of a gated tunnel opposite the King's House Hotel. An open-air café opposite the Hotel Liman is celebrated for its 'loving trees': some 200 years old, the male and female trees grow entwined together and their branches fuse.

To the east of the old town, down a track which starts from behind the Akçiçek hospital, is an area which was used as a quarry and inhabited by early Christians expelled from the town; here a tunnel leads to the rock-cut chapel of Ayia Mavra, which returns faint traces of frescoes.

On the western edge of town is the **Fine Arts Museum** (Güzel Sanatlar Muzesi), reached down Paşabahçe Sok., which leads past the military hospital and culminates in a barracks. The museum is housed in a lavish and pleasant villa built by a wealthy Briton in the 1930s, with a balcony and an airy upper terrace enjoying what must then have been uninterrupted views of the mountains and coastline. It contains European paintings (mostly unlabelled), Oriental *objets d'art*, embroideries and porcelain – there is nothing Cypriot. The museum is open daily, 08.30–17.00.

Excursions from Girne

ST HILARION

Spectacularly sited in its craggy eyrie 2,400 feet (732 m) above the plain, St Hilarion's crumbling walls and towers have inspired previous visitors to romantic effusion. Rose

St Hilarion, impregnable on its dramatic pinnacle

Macaulay's description of the place as 'a picture-book castle for elf kings' is much quoted: it is even said that the castle provided inspiration for the animators of Walt Disney's *Snow White*. The castle is indeed marvellous, but thoughts of fairy tales are whimsically inappropriate: the ruins convey strength, even cruelty, as much as romance, a strength demonstrated as recently as 1964 when a group of young Turks seized and held the castle, using it to great effect to command the main Girne–Lefkoşa road.

Originally a monastery and known as Didymus from the twin peaks over which it sprawls, the castle of St Hilarion was first fortified by the Byzantines and named for a hermit who fled from the Arab invasion of the Holy Land. It was surrendered to Richard I by Isaac Comnenos in 1191, and greatly reinforced by the Lusignans in the 1220s. For four years possession of the castle was a major bone of contention between Jean d'Ibelin, regent for the child king Henri I, and the Holy Roman Emperor Frederick II, who sought to exert control over Cyprus; eventually the young king himself defeated the Emperor at Ağirdağ (Aghirda) a few miles to the south and ended Frederick's ambitions for ever. Thereafter the Lusignans spent large sums enhancing the castle and it became half fortress and half palace; luxurious apartments were added, and the castle was regularly used as a summer residence by the royal family. In 1373, the Genoese invasion forced John, Prince of Antioch, acting as regent for the young king Pierre II, to seek refuge in the castle, an episode which led to an infamous chapter in its history: deceived by his sister-in-law (and subsequent murderer), Eleanor of Aragon, into the false belief that his Bulgarian bodyguard intended treachery, he had them led one by one to the highest point of the walls and thrown to their deaths.

The Venetians, a century later, lacked the manpower to maintain the castle, which they considered unsuited to modern warfare; they therefore 'slighted' it, to prevent it from falling into hostile hands. Despite their dismantling, however, St Hilarion remains the best preserved of the Crusader castles in Cyprus and a notable monument of medieval architecture.

The castle is open from 08.30–17.00 daily, and is reached by turning right off the main Lefkoşa road as it crosses the col about 3 miles (5 km) south of Girne. The first section of the St Hilarion road is controlled because of the proximity of the important Yaman Kişlası military camp which hides behind the hills above Girne: no stopping or photography is allowed until it has been safely passed. Shortly afterwards the metalled road passes the Lusignan tilting yard and bears right for the car park by the castle entrance.

St Hilarion consists of three distinct sections on different levels. Except for the outer walls, which though much restored are largely Byzantine, most of what you see was constructed in the 13th century. The lower ward, mainly used to quarter troops and their horses, is entered through a double gateway adorned with carved corbels: to the left is a barbican, beside which a stepped path leads past vaulted stables and a small cistern to the left to reach the gatehouse of the middle ward, once defended by a drawbridge. From here the full extent of the original Byzantine walls can be seen to the south and west, reinforced with nine round towers. A vaulted tunnel leads into the *enceinte*, from which steps lead to a ruined late 10th-century Byzantine church, originally containing four columns which supported a dome. Possibly part of the original monastery, this was used by the Lusignans as the royal chapel; in the 1950s the church was partially restored to prevent the collapse of the eastern wall. The passage continues to a large refectory, now used as a café (serving most welcome fresh orange juice), and on, past three barrack rooms, to a vaulted loggia and belvedere offering magnificent views of the countryside over 2,200 feet (700 metres) below. Next to the banqueting hall is a kitchen block, its chimneys still visible, and to the right are the original royal apartments (though the Lusignans later removed themselves to the higher level of the castle).

This upper ward is reached up a steep path (stout shoes recommended), leading westwards from the restaurant along the face of the crag and past an enormous open reservoir, which must have held enough water to last the

The Tower of Prince John

inhabitants for many months. Veer right at the top to enter the upper *enceinte* through a Frankish arch. To the north of the entrance are more kitchens and at the far (west) end of the upper plateau a long narrow building which formed the royal apartments; on the upper floor is the elegant 'Queen's window', retaining some of the original tracery and benches (reached by steps and a path to the right as you approach the apartments).

From this eyrie fine views of Karaman, the mountains and, in the distance, the Koruçam peninsula can be enjoyed. To the south, the energetic may climb the steep flight of worn steps to the Tower of Prince John, the highest section of the wall, whence the unfortunate Bulgars are thought to have been hurled to their deaths.

The harbour at Girne
The gymnasium at Salamis

Eryngium amethystinum near Iskele

Oleander in May, Lapta

Sea daffodil ('Famagusta lily')

Roller © *Eric and David Hosking*

Crested lark © *Eric and David Hoski*

The starred agama always looks alert

Bellapais

The ruins of the glorious abbey of Bellapais are reached by a turning to the right (signposted for Doğanköy and Beylerbeyi) off the main coastal road in the eastern outskirts of Girne. The road soon leaves the town to climb a hillside on which the remains of the Early Bronze Age necropolis of **Vounous**, much ruined and despoiled by tomb robbers, lie scattered; the lofty north wall of the abbey complex soon appears on your left. The village, reached after about 3 miles (5 km), risks becoming a congested tourist trap and is threatened by the encroachment of some unlovely new buildings on the outskirts, including a holiday village. It is memorably celebrated (as Bellapaix) by the late Lawrence Durrell, who lived here in a converted Turkish house from 1953–55, in his book *Bitter Lemons* (1957), an account by turns hilarious and depressing of his time on Cyprus which is required reading for every visitor to the island. He wrote his novel *Justine* here as well as entertaining friends such as Patrick Leigh Fermor, Freya Stark, George Seferis and Rose Macaulay.

The best time to visit the village is probably early on a weekday morning, in order to avoid the throngs. The abbey (open 08.00–19.00 daily) is an outstanding monument of Gothic architecture, imposingly situated on a rocky escarpment projecting from the mountainside. The Abbaye de la Paix was founded *c.* 1200 by Aimery de Lusignan, for the Augustine monks forced to leave their Church of the Holy Sepulchre in Jerusalem by the Saracens; they later accepted

The cloisters at Bellapais

the Norbertine rule, and the abbey was thereafter sometimes called the White Abbey from the colour of their
habits. King Hugues III (1267–1284) was a major benefac-
tor of the abbey, which grew in size and importance (to the
extent that the archbishop of Nicosia had trouble asserting
his authority over it), until the Genoese invasion of 1373; in
that year its treasures (which were said to have included a
fragment of the True Cross) were looted, and the abbey
never regained its previous glory. Under the Venetians the
abbey declined further, both in prosperity and morality: by
the 16th century it is recorded that many of the monks had
wives (in some cases more than one) and permitted only
their own offspring to apply as novices. The Turks sacked
the buildings in 1570, and subsequently stone from the site
was taken away to build the village which grew up around
the ruins.

The entrance is to the south-west, through an arched and
fortified gateway where there was once a drawbridge.
Immediately opposite is the oldest part of the abbey, the
well-preserved 13th-century **church**, a fine example of the
Frankish Gothic style which (like the abbey as a whole) may
strike the northern European visitor as looking incongruous
in this Levantine setting. Usually kept locked, the church
has a vaulted interior with two aisles and a nave showing
traces of frescoes. A staircase leads from the north transept
to the dormitories. Beyond the church lie the 14th-century
cloisters, still beautiful although the surrounding arcades
have gone and only fragments of the delicate arches which
supported them remain. The carved bosses and corbels of
the vaulting feature human and animal heads, rosettes and
Lusignan coats of arms, and in the north-west corner is a
large marble sarcophagus of the 2nd century AD which the
monks used as a wash basin. To the north is the magnificent
refectory, the abbey's chief glory. The marble lintel above
the door bears carvings of the arms of Jerusalem, the
Lusignans and of Cyprus (a combination of the other two).

The **refectory**'s interior is pure Gothic and some 90 ft
(27 m) long with six fine vaulted bays. Along the walls can
be seen the marks where the monks' benches were, with a
higher bench under the small rose window at the eastern end
for the abbot; from the northern wall juts a decorative
pulpit, reached by steps built within the thickness of the
wall, from which the monks would have heard edifying
readings while they ate. The windows in this wall have a
superb outlook down the coast. Incredibly, the British used
this glorious hall as a rifle range, but the building has
nevertheless survived intact.

From the western end of the refectory steps lead down to

The Tree of Idleness, whose shadow 'incapacitates one for serious work'

a pillared **undercroft**, lit by arrow slits, which was used for storage; above are the kitchen block at the north-western corner and the ruined *cellarium* (store rooms) running down the side of the cloister. On the far side of the cloisters is the **chapterhouse**, with the remains of the stone benches on which the canons sat and some lively carvings on the corbels in the walls. The single pillar standing in the centre once supported the roof: it probably came from Lambousa. Above the plain barrel-vaulted undercroft or common room next to it, with a rose window at the northern end, were the **dormitories**, of which only one wall survives, with a window and a storage niche for each monk. Returning to the cloisters, staircases on the southern side give access to the roof (and provide an opportunity to peer through a window into the church). The views from here are stupendous, and one can inspect the belfry and also view the chapterhouse and undercroft from above; on top of the north aisle of the church is a small vaulted treasury.

Lovers of *Bitter Lemons* may find the surrounding village disappointing. The Tree of Idleness, an ancient mulberry, still shades customers at the café near the abbey entrance – opposite is a café restaurant which has appropriated its name and sports a superb jacaranda through which steps to the balcony are ingeniously entwined. Durrell's house can be found a little way up the hill: a plaque commemorates his residence here, but the house is unrecognisable otherwise, having been extensively reconstructed by a later British owner. Steep narrow streets are, however, still a feature of the village and perhaps one can just imagine Frangos driving his protesting cattle pell mell down them.

Behind the village a minor road crosses the flank of Mt Komando (Alonagra); the maze of tracks through the woods provide good walking but it is all too easy to get lost.

Buffavento

Least accessible of the Crusader castles, Buffavento, wind-buffeted as its name implies, is also the highest, perched on a dizzy crag of some 3,100 feet (940 m). Called the Castle of the Lion by medieval chroniclers, its origins are something of a mystery, since most of its architectural features cannot be dated. Some Byzantine brickwork is visible, and it is known that 'the exceeding strong castle of Buffevent' existed in 1191, when it was surrendered to Richard the Lionheart by Isaac Comnenos' daughter. Pierre I, the idealistic Lusignan king who sought to revive the crusading spirit but became embittered by his failure, found an unpleasant use for the castle: he imprisoned his loyal friend Sir John Visconti there as a punishment for warning him of Queen Eleanor's infidelity, and allowed him to starve to death. There are several other instances of Buffavento being used as a prison by the Lusignans, and like St Hilarion the castle was held against the Genoese by supporters of Pierre II. Like St Hilarion, too, it was slighted by the Venetians, who removed its artillery and much of its roof. Accounts by

Buffavento, 'blown by the winds'

17th-century visitors make much of the difficult and dangerous ascent and report seeing great numbers of ruined chambers, suggesting that the complex must once have been very large.

Maps of North Cyprus suggest that there are several roads to Buffavento, but the area around Güngör to the south is reserved for the military and any attempt to approach the castle from the south or the west will result in frustration. The only way is to proceed eastwards along the coast road from Girne, which turns inland after 6 miles (9½ km) and climbs towards the blade-like crags of Mt Beşparmak (Pentadaktylos) to a pass between Beşparmak and the vertical cliffs which terminate the next section of the range. (This is a controlled road and forbidden to UN vehicles: no photography is permitted from it.) At the top of the pass a rough track leads to the right along the ridge to a parking area by a rusting sign announcing '*Bufavento Kalesi*'. From here the walk to the castle far above, its sandier masonry just distinguishable from the rock out of which it seems to grow, takes 30–40 minutes. (Vehicles with four-wheel drive can climb a little further on, cutting 10 minutes off the walk, to another parking area around an olive tree where there is a marble memorial to the passengers and crew of a plane which tragically clipped the top of the mountains on its approach to Ercan in February 1988 and plummeted to its destruction on the steep slopes below.)

The walk up the cliff is steep but not as arduous as it looks from below; there is a well-defined path and plenty of interest on the way. Birds wheel above and below you (hooded crows, vultures and even hoopoes), and butterflies and innumerable lizards offer frequent excuses for a welcome pause. Breathtaking views open up below you as you climb: the villages of the Mesarya plain appear laid out like a map, with Lefkoşa baking in the haze in the centre and the tumbled Troodos on the horizon. A single enormous cypress between you and the large army camp below marks the site of the important monastery of **Ayios Chrysostomos**, unhappily inaccessible within the camp precincts. As you breast the ridge, more aerial views appear, of the north coast now, and all the way up the Kirpaşa peninsula.

Soon after this the Lusignan **gatehouse** is reached: Greek and Turkish graffiti mingle indiscriminately within, an iron gate hangs open and someone has chalked 'Wellcome' on the wall. Beyond are various rooms, one of them built over a vaulted cistern (water storage would have been an important consideration for the garrison) and a balcony with views down the range to the west; St Hilarion is plainly visible – Buffavento could communicate with both St

Sunday picnickers at Alevkaya

Hilarion and Kantara to the east by means of bonfires. Beyond, steep steps lead to a **watchtower** with an arched tiled entrance, built over another cistern, and higher still is the upper ward, at the very top of the crag: here are the remains of a church and other buildings, and a platform offering vertiginous views of the north coast.

Sourp Magar, Alevkaya and Antiphonitis

To reach the beautiful and remote monastery of Antiphonitis, follow the same route from Girne as for Buffavento, but at the crest of the pass turn left onto a rough and rocky track signposted for the Alevkaya Herbarium.

This track passes beneath the south face of **Mt Beşparmak**, with a close-up view of its spectacular pinnacles. A distinctive landmark in the Girne range, the mountain is 2,429 feet (740 m) high and when seen from the coast very much resembles the fist which gives it its name in both Turkish and Greek – legend has it that it was formed by the handprint of Dighenis, the Byzantine hero, when he grasped the peak after leaping across the sea from Asia Minor to escape his Arab enemies. Beyond it, the track crawls along the northern slopes of the range with grandiose views.

After about 4½ miles (7 km) the roofless remains of the monastery of **Sourp Magar** can be made out below the road; founded in *c.* 1000 and originally Coptic, the monastery passed to the Armenians in the 15th century and was an important pilgrimage destination prior to 1974. Shortly afterwards a metalled road is reached at the forestry station of **Alevkaya** (Halevga); here there are large clearings in the pine woods – it is an extremely popular spot for the barbecues and picnics of which the Cypriots are so fond at weekends, when the woods are filled with lively parties cooking, drinking, dancing and relaxing in the shade. Down the road a little to the right can be found the **North Cyprus Herbarium** (*see p. 40*), with a fascinating collection of samples and illustrations of native North Cypriot botanical species.

For Antiphonitis, however, turn left on the metalled road, which descends in short tight turns past the turning for Karaağac and makes its way along a ledge halfway up the mountain through glorious forest scenery. A few miles on, the metalled road bends sharply left for Esentepe, but our route diverges onto a rough track (not recommended after rain) continuing east and skirting several deep ravines. After almost three miles of this a crossroads is reached; the 12th-century monastery lies down to the left, but the track here is so bad that even 4-wheeled drive vehicles should hesitate. It is best to park the car here and walk down (10–15 minutes) to the monastery which nestles in a cleft in the hills.

The octagonal domed church of **Antiphonitis** ('Christ of the Echo') contains some of the few examples of frescoes to be seen in North Cyprus; many have been stolen or defaced, but enough survive to make the visit well worth making. The paintings in the sanctuary are Byzantine and date from the late 12th century: in the apse the Virgin Mary is depicted flanked by the Archangels Gabriel and Michael dressed in

The simple 12th-century monastery church of Antiphonitis; the Gothic loggia beside it and the western porch (narthex) are later additions

the uniform of ushers to the Byzantine court and Christ appears as a medallion. The south wall was decorated with a large representation of the Tree of Jesse, now mostly looted, but a column at the south-west corner has a well-preserved Baptism scene and there is an interesting 15th-century fresco of the birth of the Virgin (depicted lying in a box) in which the realistic perspective of the background shows the influence of the Renaissance. The inside of the dome is covered by a splendid 15th-century medallion of Christ Pantocrator with the Apostles seated on thrones around. Eight columns support the dome, four of them detached and four built onto the walls. Outside, the elegant arched loggia beside the church (once roofed) is a Frankish addition dating from the 15th century.

From the monastery return to the crossroads and drive back to the metalled road: about halfway along you may spot the simple monastery church of **Apati** above the road, hidden from view on the outward journey. At the junction, a right turn brings you down to the village of **Esentepe** where the coast road back to Girne can be joined (*see p. 101*).

Karaman (Karmi)

This pretty village is reached by a turning inland from the centre of Karaoğlanoğlu. Popular with expatriates, mostly British and Germans, the village has been 'done up' as the result of an enlightened government policy which grants long leases on abandoned properties to foreigners willing to restore them while paying a nominal rent (it is planned that Ilgaz, a similarly sited village to the west, will soon benefit from this forward-looking treatment). Situated high up on the northern slopes of the Beşparmak range with magnificent views, the village is pleasantly cool in summer, but suffers from a loss of sunlight early in the day: indeed in winter, when the population reduces to a few dozen, it scarcely sees the sun at all. On the way up to Karaman, below Edremit, the road passes the **church of Panayia Chrysotrimithios,** of which the apse is formed by the tiny original Byzantine chapel; and just below the drive to the Duckworth House restaurant, a small sign points to a **Bronze Age cemetery**, in an enclosure reached by a path from the end of the metalled road. Tomb 6 (roofed over) contains an unusual feature – a weathered and rudimentary relief of what may be a fertility goddess in the *dromos* (approach), the earliest funerary relief on the island; the lintel of the entrance is carved to imitate a doorway. Dating from *c.* 1900–1800 BC, this necropolis is earlier than the Royal Tombs at Salamis; a Minoan-style cup was found in one of the tombs, as well as some blue beads thought to have come from Egypt.

Entering Karaman there is parking near the church, which is opened every Sunday from 10.00–13.00 only by a lady resident who has lived here for over twenty years: it is well-preserved and retains its iconostasis though none of the icons is older than the 19th century. Almost entirely populated by foreigners, with a 'High Street' and houses with names such as 'Cobblers', Karaman nevertheless has genuine charm. Picturesque corners abound and there is a pub, the Crow's Nest, a couple of restaurants and an art gallery.

Panayia Absinthiotissa

This remote and picturesquely sited monastery stands on a plateau almost 1700 feet (510 m) high to the north of the village of Taşkent, reached via the largely abandoned village of Kaynakköy and Aşağı Dikmen. These villages, lying south of the Beşparmak range, can be approached either from the main Girne–Lefkoşa road or by one of several roads heading north over the plain from the dual carriage-way north of the capital. The hillside above them is boldly inscribed with a North Cyprus flag and Atatürk's proud slogan *'Ne Mutlu Türküm Diyene'* (How fortunate is the man who can say 'I am a Turk') for the benefit of any northward-gazing Greeks.

The people of **Taşkent**, originally the Maronite village of Vouno with a church dedicated to the 4th-century martyr St Romanos, are mainly refugees from the south who suffered badly in the troubled years before 1974. A small building on an eminence in the village houses the martyrs' museum, commemorating members of the Turkish community who died when their village was attacked by EOKA in December 1963: the display includes horrific pictures of the exhumation of the bound victims from a mass grave by the Red Cross the following year.

A metalled road leads north from the village shop, up which, after about 550 yards (500 m), a rough track goes off to the right before the entrance to a commercial gravel pit, bearing right again opposite a water tower; just around the next corner a further track leads directly to the plateau on which the monastery stands, with Buffavento's soaring crag visible to the right. (Vehicles with four-wheel drive can negotiate the track all the way to the monastery, but hired cars are best left near the metalled road, from which it is a pleasant uphill stroll to the site, the peace of the setting enhanced by the melodious tinkling of goat bells on the hillsides.) The track passes various outbuildings (on one of which the slogan 'Cyprus is Greek' can still be read) with delightful views of the monastery church nestling beneath the wall of the mountains. Around the plateau concrete Greek sentry boxes forlornly command the plain below.

The monastery church (once known as the Abbey of Abscithi) is originally Byzantine, but was partially remodelled in the Gothic style in the 15th century and restored in the 1960s, and is still in good structural repair. The murals which adorned the narthex have been stolen and the entrance is blocked with rough barriers against the sheep, but one can clamber in to view the peeling remains of a few defaced frescoes and the vaulting at the west end. North of the church are numerous outbuildings, and more line the track beyond, which eventually peters out against the mountain (where some inscribed graffiti, high above your head, provoke speculation as to the motives and sanity of the intrepid perpetrators!). Clearly the monastery was once the centre of a sizeable community.

Eastwards from here a minor road follows the contours of the hills, but further progress is prohibited outside Güngör, which lies within a military area: unfortunately this forbidden zone also includes the important Byzantine monastery of **Ayios Chrysostomos** and the large ruined church of **Panayia Koutsovendis**.

Mountain Drive

A forestry road (built by the British at a cost, it is said, of £300 per mile) runs from St Hilarion westwards all the way to the end of the Beşparmak range and offers an excellent opportunity to drink in some spectacular views or to ramble in the mountains, enjoying the butterflies and flowers. The track is of variable quality but perfectly negotiable with care in a hired car for its entire length. It is probably safest avoided, however, when there has been recent heavy rain.

The track begins at **St Hilarion** (see above), where it bears left from the metalled road, climbing to a viewpoint from which there are splendid views of the castle perched on its crag and of the plain to the south; the village of Ağirdağ lies directly below, with Pınarbaşı and Dağyolu beyond; the Lefkoşa road knifes across the plain to disappear, often, in haze, while to your right looms the bulk of the Troodos mountains. From here onwards, occasional tracks to either side of the road invite exploration on foot, offering the opportunity to stretch your legs and stroll through the pines for further views to either side of the range; wild sage and thick carpets of cistus scent the air. Some two miles (3 km) further on the road passes above Karaman and to the right Girne harbour is distantly visible. Fork right when presented with a choice and soon **Mt Selvili** (Kyparissovouno), at 3357 feet (1023 m) the highest peak in the range, comes into view ahead, crowned with a red and white pylon. Passing an abandoned sentry box and a few derelict houses the road descends, bringing the Troodos into full view, then climbs again. The views to the north now feature the prominent bulk of Asil Nadir's uncompleted Crystal Cove Hotel, also Alsancak and the Akhiropiitos monastery by the shore.

After about 6 miles (9½ km), a crossroads is reached, with a sign that seems to have been used for target practice; to the left here a track in poor condition skirts the mountains to the south and overlooks the plain, towards which it descends quite rapidly past a quarry to reach lower ground at the village of **Akçiçek** in about 20 minutes. A right turn here winds down similarly to the north reaching **Lapta** via the Başpınar restaurant after about 4 miles (6½ km). For more splendid mountain scenery, however, go straight on at the crossroads: this track, usually deserted save for a profusion of birds, butterflies and lizards and the occasional melodiously tinkling goat, winds around the northern flank of Mt Selvili with stupendous views back along the coast (photography forbidden as you pass the turning for the pylon), before traversing a small pass and emerging on the southern flanks of **Mt Kıvanç** (Kornos). Just before the pass, a damaged tank has lain abandoned since 1974, poised at an improbable angle down the slope where it stuck while manoeuvring to outflank resistance at Lapta. The Troodos

Looking down on Karaman from the forest road

mountains and the plain come once again into view, with the low ridge of hills around Kalkanlı, then suddenly the whole of the Koruçam peninsula appears to the west. The last stretch of the track is the least stable and needs care: it descends beneath the soaring peak of Mt Kıvanç (3148 feet, 960 m) to reach a metalled road. Here turn right through pleasant wooded scenery for **Karşıyaka**, where bearing left by the church, then right, will bring you down to the coast road. Although only some 18 miles (29 km) one should allow at least 1½ hours for this drive, or more if you take time to admire the views.

EAST FROM GIRNE

From the City Hall roundabout, the road east passes in turn
the post office, the hospital, the National Archive and the
turning for Doğanköy and Beylerbeyi (Bellapais, *see p. 87*).
Immediately after this junction the English cemetery lies on
the left, behind a desecrated Greek one, just before the
approach road to the modern harbour. About a mile out of
town is the village of **Karakum**: here a turning by the Hong
Kong Chinese restaurant leads to a rocky foreshore where a
right turn along a dirt track brings you to a small horseshoe-
shaped cove of gently shelving sand, perfect for young
children. Bellapais Abbey is prominent on the right of the
road as it approaches **Çatalköy**, a prosperous village set on
a ridge; some of the houses are built on top of caves in the
rock, as is the 19th-century church (now a mosque) of Ayios
Epiktitos, who lived as a hermit in a cave beneath the
building.

On the left after the Çatalköy turning is an army base,
which incorporates a collapsing chapel and a large villa
(presumably Fortuna, the house whose building for Lawrence Durrell's friend is described in *Bitter Lemons*). Just
beyond it a minor road leads to a windswept promontory on
which the **Tekke (Dervish Convent) of Hazaret Ömer**
stands beside the sea. This shrine, recently restored, is
venerated by Greek and Turkish Cypriots alike as the burial
place of seven Moslem saints. Six miles (9½ km) from
Girne, just before the main road swings inland, an enormous sign announces the Barış Plaj (Peace Beach), reserved
for soldiers. At this junction, bear left along the coast,
following signs for Esentepe. This road, completely rebuilt
in 1991, immediately passes the Acapulco development – a
hotel and apartments built around an attractive, sandy
beach with all facilities to which visitors are admitted for a
reasonable charge. The grounds incorporate the Neolithic
site of **Vrysi**, apparently abandoned at the beginning of the
4th millennium BC; in the north-eastern corner of the site a
settlement was excavated in 1969–74, consisting of single-
roomed stone huts partially sunk into the ground, which
yielded quantities of boldly painted pottery.

Two miles further on lies **Lara beach**, which has a snack
bar, as well as showers, changing rooms, umbrellas and
sunbeds for hire. The beach is sandy with enormous ribs of

sunbeds for hire. The beach is sandy with enormous ribs of smooth sandstone at the western end, looking a little like beached whales; here rock pools form and the rocks provide excellent opportunities for sunbathing, diving or just exploring. There are curious formations in the cliff behind, with caves and protruding knobs of rock resembling a giant's playground. Shortly after the Lara turning a sign to the right points to the remote village of **Beşparmak** (Trapeza) in the shadow of the mountain of the same name. Abandoned in the 1960s, the village has now been resettled by a handful of families; the road up to it is extremely scenic, winding through a landscape of strangely flat-topped hills and past many empty houses of mellow old stone, which provide shade for the sheep.

A feature of this part of the coast is the rock pinnacles, sometimes mushroom-capped with loose boulders, which stand at the ends of many of the bays and coves, the result of the natural erosion of limestone blocks which have become separated from the land. One such frames the end of the next bay, where North Cyprus' power station is being built, and another stands guard over **Alakati Beach**, which follows. Here there are signs of development, but the beach is shingly and exposed to winds and seaweed infestation. A far better bathing place, indeed one of the finest beaches in North Cyprus, lies just beyond it, the so-called **'Turtle Beach'** or 'Twelve Mile Beach East', backed by an immense area of dunes. To reach it, drive past St Kathleen's restaurant as far as a sharp bend immediately after a small bridge; here a rough track to the left leads to the western end of the bay, bearing right through the dunes to a parking area. This is a long beach of perfect sand, divided in two by a long spit, which offers excellent bathing. There are no facilities and no shade, and you may well find you have its entire length to yourself. There are other routes to the beach: just under 2 miles further on, after the road has made two long sweeps inland towards Mt Beşparmak, a gap in the fence on the left gives access to a headland from which a steep descent can be made to the eastern end. Here there is a notice warning visitors not to disturb the turtles which breed here in the summer. To the east of this headland is a further beach, slightly horseshoe-shaped with castle-like rock formations at the western end, and to the east an enormous vertical slab like a menhir. The low red buildings nearby represent the beginnings of an intended holiday village, but the difficulties presently being experienced by its developers, Polly Peck International, suggest it may not achieve completion for some time.

The road winds on between the mountains and the sea,

reaching after 4 miles (7 km) the turning for **Karaağaç**. Half-a-mile before a small chapel by the seashore a track leads onto a headland which is strewn with potsherds from an ancient site; the larger stones were all removed to build the medieval village, but to the west is a necropolis in which several rock-cut tombs are visible (one with a face roughly carved on it) and on the shingle beach below, which was once the harbour, you can find traces of a stone jetty. Shortly after this the village of **Esentepe** appears on a ridge ahead: opposite the turning to it stands a large 19th-century structure which was used for storing carobs, an important export of the area. It is possible to drive up through Esentepe and take a track to the left (where the road bends sharply right above the village) to see the remote 12th-century monastery church of **Antiphonitis** (*see p. 93–4*).

A couple of miles further on, on a double bend, a track to the left leads onto **Cape Dik** (Stazouza): here the cape shelters a small harbour, a valuable haven of calm water for sailors off this coast. Behind it stand a few ruined hovels and, on either side of the track leading to them, groups of large stones suggest that there may once have been a Neolithic settlement here. The road next passes the overgrown 15th-century monastery church of **Melandryna** with flying buttresses added in the 18th century, and the turning for Bahçeli – sited, like all the villages along this vulnerable coast, on higher ground a short distance inland as a protection against seaborne raiders. The conical peak of Mt Ziya (Olympos, 2427 ft, 740 m) appears ahead as the road approaches **Küçükerenköy**, with a small shingly beach protected by a natural sandstone breakwater and popular with fishermen; a decaying hotel here suggests that there were once hopes of turning this into a resort. This area of North Cyprus is dedicated to market gardening: salad crops, courgettes, beans and other vegetables are grown in plastic-covered greenhouses and the beds of the many streams which the road has to negotiate are often intensively cultivated. Drive straight on at the junction with the mountain road to Geçitkale and Gazimağusa which joins the coast road here and continue to a T-junction: a right turn here leads to the ancient village of **Tatlisu** (petrol station), but the coastal route goes to the left, passing the ruins of **Aphrodision**, which may have been the Hittite capital of the island *c.* 700 BC: they have been much plundered for building materials and do not repay a visit.

More interesting is the area around a small chapel, now used as a barn, which stands beyond the ubiquitous greenhouses some way off the road to the left about 3 miles (5 km) further on. Nearby are rock-cut chambers and the most cursory inspection of the fields around reveals a positive litter of broken pottery fragments, tiles and other remains from yet another ancient settlement, probably **Pergamos**. Inland lies the medieval church of **Panayia Pergamiotissa**, once completely frescoed, with a small chapel cut into the rock nearby and more ruins of an ancient village. Here the coastline is rocky with only occasional stretches of sand, and the route soon turns inland towards Mersinlik, Kantara and Iskele by a large arched building which was presumably another carob store. The road climbs the flanks of **Mt Sinan** (2374 feet, 724 m), greener and not as high as the peaks to the west of the range, but nevertheless spectacular, with limestone pinnacles and knife-edged crags rising from forests of pine and arbutus. Views of the sea to the south suddenly appear and the road curves left round elaborately terraced hills to reach the small pine-shaded village of **Kantara**, a cool resort in summer. Here drive straight on for the castle, some 2½ miles (4 km) to the east.

Kantara Castle

The easternmost of the three great Crusader castles of Cyprus, Kantara is also the lowest; its siting is nevertheless impressive, perched above sheer cliffs on three sides, and affording breathtaking views up the Kirpaşa peninsula, over Famagusta bay to the south and, on clear days, even across to mainland Turkey and Syria.

Kantara (its name is the Arabic for 'bridge') was first fortified in the late 9th century, and like the other Byzantine strongholds was surrendered to Richard the Lionheart by the usurper Isaac Comnenos. Like them also, Kantara was strengthened by the Lusignan kings in the late 13th century and played a part in resisting the Genoese invasion in 1373, after the boy king's uncle and regent, Prince John of Antioch, escaped there following the loss of Famagusta – assisted by his cook, he managed to flee his dungeon by disguising himself as a potboy. In 1391 the castle was further refortified under Jacques I, but the Venetians slighted it in 1525 as they did Buffavento and St Hilarion: their defensive strategy placed more reliance on the massive new walls they had built around Kyrenia, Nicosia and Famagusta than on these fairy tale medieval castles which pre-dated the age of gunpowder. Nevertheless, considerable portions of Kantara's graceful outer walls remain to be admired today.

The road ends beside the least precipitous, eastern side of the castle. From a parking area a winding path leads towards the outer wall: its powerful fortifications are quite well-preserved and the small round towers still retain their battlements. The entrance to the castle (incongruously signalled by a plaque commemorating an International Urological Congress) is through an impressive but ruined **barbican** defended by two square towers; inside, a **bailey** must be crossed before reaching the entrance to the main *enceinte*. To the right a corridor with loopholes leads to the two-storey **north-east tower**, with more defensive loopholes in the metre-thick walls and an unusual elongated turret. Left of the main entrance, the **south-eastern tower** contains a square chamber with an *oubliette* or cistern beneath, which was used as a prison. Next to it are three vaulted rooms with arrow slits which provided accommodation for the garrison: at the end of the block is a medieval latrine, flushed by a channel which brought water from the castle's quite elaborate plumbing system. Continuing clockwise round the site, a horseshoe-shaped cistern can be seen and at the western edge of the castle, past a demolished section of the walls, are three more vaulted rooms and a postern gate from which the defenders could emerge to take a besieging force by surprise. Another tower on the highest point of the site preserves a Gothic window and offers panoramic views: from here beacon messages could be transmitted to Buffavento and on to St Hilarion, Kyrenia and Nicosia.

Return to the village and turn left following signs for Turnalar and Gazimağusa. The road gently descends the southern slopes of the mountains with fine views over the eastern end of the Mesarya plain. **Turnalar**, at the mountains' base, is a small farming village of mudbrick

Well-preserved towers flank the entrance to Kantara castle

houses with a crumbling church which, although danger-ously leaning, retains an iron cross on top of its belfry. Head through the village on a poor road to **Yarköy**, another rather run-down hamlet, where the women wear traditional Turkish dress. As you approach the coast there are more and more cornfields until, bearing left in Boğaztepe, you enter **Boğaz**, traditionally a Turkish settlement and one of the few fishing villages in North Cyprus. Here there are two hotels, numerous restaurants and a small beach next to the little harbour.

> At Boğaz you have a number of alternatives: the choice will depend on how much of the day is left. If time permits, carry on along the coast to Salamis and Famagusta (*see pp 137–8*), whence you can return to Girne along the fast road across the plain which bypasses Lefkoşa.
>
> Alternatively take the opportunity to explore a little way along the Kirpaşa peninsula (*see p. 149*) – the coast road back to Girne can be regained by turning north through **Tuzluca** and **Büyükkonuk** 4 miles (6 km) north-east of Boğaz. This road passes through pretty countryside, skirting the eastern end of the mountains with fine views of Kantara and the coast, which is reached near the ancient site of **Galounia**. It then passes **Kaplıca**, just beyond the turning to which there is an excellent sandy beach, usually deserted despite the provision of a bar and changing facilities. Continuing westwards a small shingly cove is passed, distinguished by curious stalactite curtains caused by water dripping over the limestone cliff, and the road runs along a pebbly foreshore interspersed with areas of limestone pavement to reach the Mersinlik/Kantara turning once more.

Those whose time is short but nevertheless wish to return to Girne without retracing their steps may make their way back through a succession of Mesarya villages to the south of the mountains. This involves driving south from Boğaz to a crossroads, signposted Iskele and Geçitkale, at which you turn right.

Iskele (Trikomo), reached down a quiet road, is famous for pomegranates and infamous for being the home village of the EOKA leader General Grivas. In the central square stands a tiny sunken church, the Dominican chapel of **Ayios Iakovos** (mostly 15th century, but restored in 1804), a charming miniature which so appealed to Queen Marie of Romania that she had a replica of it built as her family chapel on the shores of the Black Sea. Leaving the village for Geçitkale the church of the **Panayia Theotokos** to the left of the road, a domed 12th-century building, has been restored and reopened in 1991 as an **Icon Museum**. Most of the icons on display are modern, but several frescoes

The little chapel of Ayios Iakovos, Iskele

survive to be admired: around the southern recess these are
12th century, as is the large painting of Christ in the dome;
those in the north aisle (a later addition to the church) are
Frankish-Byzantine. They include part of an Ascension and
date from the 15th century. One of the carved marble panels
from the original Byzantine iconostasis is preserved built
into the belfry.

This rural road continues past several typical Mesaryan
agricultural villages, where in summer flocks of sheep and
goats browse among the barley stalks, often tended by
children or very old gentlemen. Akova (Gypsos – the Greek
name deriving from the gypsum deposits nearby) is passed,
then **Geçitkale** (petrol), a scruffy settlement on an important crossroads, and the site of the Republic's second
airport, at present little used. The town used to be famous
for its weaving. Hereafter the road gets rougher and
narrower, passing through the villages of **Sütlüce** and
Gönendere and finally reaching the large township of
Değirmenlik (Kythrea) after some 27 miles (43½ km). An
agglomeration of several villages sited south of the important ancient site of **Khytri** (a Greek foundation of *c.* 1200
BC), there was a Neolithic settlement here from about 3500
BC. For centuries the area has depended on a stream which
issues from the mountains nearby: aqueducts once con-
veyed its water to Salamis, and in the medieval period it
drove numerous flour mills which ground corn for Nicosia
as well as watering extensive cotton plantations around the
village. Değirmenlik is also said to be the place from which
the cauliflower was introduced to Europe in 1604. There are
several churches in the village, the most ancient being the

Maronite chapel of St Andronikos: north of the village is the Monastery of the Panayia (1771).

From Değirmenlik the road heads north and makes a left–right dogleg to join the main military-controlled road which runs past limestone quarries back to Girne across the pass between Mt Beşparmak and Buffavento.

WEST FROM GIRNE

The busy road westwards from Girne is undergoing major improvements at the time of writing. It passes the palatial Jasmine Court Hotel, set above a small rocky beach, then a military encampment beyond which is the showroom and ceramics factory of Dizayn 74 (whose simple products are ubiquitous in the bars and restaurants of North Cyprus), before entering **Karaoğlanoğlu** (Ayios Georgios).

By the sea here is a rock-cut Byzantine chapel above the fossilized remains of many pigmy hippopotami, which the villagers used to grind up and drink as a cure for disease, believing them to be the bones of St Phanourios. Known to the British as Tiger Bay, the village's present name honours the commander who died leading the Turkish troops who landed just to the west in July 1974 (it is most easily pronounced by foreigners if taken slowly and divided into three: Kara-olan-oloo). On the eastern outskirts is a rocky beach occupied by the Riviera Bungalows, and a number of other hotels and holiday developments line the shore to the north of the village, which sprawls along the road. There are two horse-riding centres here and several supermarkets and restaurants. In the centre a turning to the left leads to Edremit and Karaman (*see pp. 94–5*).

Leaving Karaoğlanoğlu the road passes an appealingly eccentric display outside the 'Ali Nasni Borova Stone and Wood Carving World' and, beyond the Beverley Hills bungalows, the Karaoğlanoğlu Şehitleği (martyrs' monument); here, in a gravelled garden of roses, hibiscus and oleander, are the graves of 71 men who died in the 1974 landings; beside is a park displaying light tanks, lorries and landing craft, and a little further on the grandiose concrete **Peace and Freedom monument** which marks the landing place. Next to it is the popular Altınkaya fish restaurant, beside which a road leads down to **'Bambi Beach'** (properly Yavuz Çikarma Plaj) in the shadow of the monument, with excellent bathing from soft sand in shallow, very clean water; one can swim or wade out to the 'Golden Rock' in the small bay, which is the haunt of kingfishers and itself has a small south-facing beach. A little further on there is another very pleasant paying beach below the Denizkızı Hotel: here the best water sports facilities on the island are provided by Dolphin Sailing (*see p. 74*).

The 'Golden Rock' at Yavuz Çikarma beach

The next small cove along this coast is the site of the partially completed five-star Crystal Cove Hotel, one of several developments in the Republic on which work has been abandoned, pending a solution to the problems of Asil Nadir's Polly Peck International. Shortly after this a turning to the left leads to **Alsancak** (Karavas), founded in the Middle Ages from nearby Lapta (Lapithos, see below) and like it famous for its lemon trees, some of which are said to be of great age. Opposite the second turning to the village, the Mare Monte Hotel offers another paying beach. Further to the west there is a further rocky beach, prone to eel-grass infestation, with a restaurant run by soldiers.

Unhappily the large army base next to this beach incorporates within its borders two historic sites of great interest, which consequently cannot be visited. The first of these is the 12th-century **Akhiropiitos monastery** (the name means 'made without hands', from the legend that the Virgin transported the building here in a single night from Asia Minor to save it from defilement by the heathen). Rebuilt in the 14th century, the church has two domes over a central cruciform section, but was much altered in later years. The 'Shroud of Turin' is reputed to have been kept here for many years before being taken to its present resting place by a Princess of the House of Savoy. Today the army is said to use the monastery church as a warehouse and its state of repair is uncertain.

Beyond it lie the ruins of the ancient city of **Lambousa** ('the Shining One'), founded by Spartan Greeks in the 12th century BC, but later taken over by Phoenicians. The city exported pottery and reached a height of prosperity during the Roman and Byzantine periods: it was the seat of a bishop from AD 61. It was sacked by the Arabs in the 7th century, but a quantity of 6th-century silver plates etc., the 'Lambousa Treasure', escaped to be excavated in 1905. They were found near the **Chapel of Ayios Evlambios**, an unusual building worked from a single huge block of rock in the middle of a quarry, and the treasure is now divided between the Cyprus, British and Metropolitan Museums. Today there is a rifle range here and churches are surrounded by huts and bunkers roofed with corrugated iron.

A short distance further on, to the left of the road, is **Lapta** (Lapithos), a pretty village surrounded by citrus orchards – its lemons have been famous for two thousand years. The town was founded by refugees from Lambousa, driven inland by constant Arab raids, and later became an important administrative centre. (A road through Lapta, following signs to the Başpınar restaurant, connects with the mountain route described on *pp. 96–8*: bearing left onto a dirt road when the restaurant is passed will take you up the mountain, with magnificent views, to reach the crossroads described on *p. 97*.)

Opposite the Lapta turning is a track leading to a youth camp, and after this the road runs along by the sea, reaching a touristic area around the Celebrity Hotel after about a mile. Here, in addition to the Celebrity, are the Marmaris Hotel, the Club Lapethos holiday complex and the extraordinarily opulent Chateau Lambousa Hotel; there are also a number of restaurants, including the entertaining Ali Paşa's. Just beyond the hotels the excellent **L.A. Beach** offers good swimming, with umbrellas, sunbeds and a snack bar. A little further on is another restaurant, the popular **Rita on the Rocks** (with swimming pool); then the road leaves the seashore, passing through olive groves, cornfields and citrus orchards. At the next crossroads the road to the right (signposted Flamingo Motel) leads to **Güzelyalı** (Vavilas), a small fishing village in a shingly cove with a restaurant; to the left lies **Karşıyaka** (Vasilia), clinging to the lower slopes of Mt Kıvanç, the westernmost peak of the Beşparmak range: around the village lie the remains of an Early Cypriot cemetery.

Past the crossroads the road approaches the coast again near a military camp, where a small section of hard-packed sand on the rather windswept foreshore has been cleared to create a beach for the Club Güzelyalı. About 5 miles (8 km) from the Celebrity a road to the right (signposted Kayalar and Sadrazamköy) offers a diversion to Koruçam Burnu (Cape Kormakiti), the island's north-eastern extremity.

This quiet and scenic road follows the coast, ascending rapidly to become a corniche above an indented shoreline with several coves and small patches of sand to which one can clamber down for a solitary dip; this remote corner of the island is a mass of wild flowers in early spring and rewarding for birdwatchers. The impoverished-looking agricultural village of **Kayalar** is reached after about 3 miles (5 km): as their costume indicates, the inhabitants are mostly resettled emigrants from mainland Turkey. After the village the road surface improves, and 3 miles further on a steep track to the right leads onto a promontory where a curious conical outcrop of rock rears over the sea – the westernmost end of the Beşparmak range. By it stand the small chapel of Ayios Nikolaos (desecrated and now locked) and a sturdy fortified building, vaulted but roofless, which was probably a Venetian watchtower. The landscape now degenerates into tawny foothills covered with scrub and stunted trees. About 5½ miles (9 km) from Kayalar lies **Sadrazamköy**, another remote agricultural village: the 19th-century mudbrick church stands on the site of a much more ancient structure, however, and there was once a Roman temple nearby. Beyond the village the road surface deteriorates as it winds through flat scrubby country with small patches of cultivation in the red soil to reach the unmanned light on its rusting gantry at the tip of **Koruçam Burnu** (Cape Kormakiti).

This bleak spot is a mere 41 miles (66 km) from Cape Anamur, but the mainland is usually hidden from sight by haze. On the shore, the rocks clang like metal and form a curious crust over small almost perfectly circular pools. Yet this harsh and rocky environment supports an amazing variety of xerophilous rock plants – small sedums, succulents and sea daffodils: lizards are everywhere, and butterflies abound, despite the windy barrenness of the area. Until a few years ago this little-visited corner of the island was all reserved for the military, but no longer: grounds for optimism, perhaps, that other, more interesting areas that are inaccessible at present may one day be open to the visitor.

Back at Sadrazamköy, bear right past numerous abandoned houses and soon the road climbs through pinewoods, with olive groves and the occasional cornfield, before descending to a flat plain, covered with fields growing cereals. **Koruçam** (Kormakiti), the next village reached, has traditionally been the main Maronite village on Cyprus, and remains so, the Turkish liberators having declared they had no quarrel with this non-Greek Christian sect. Maronites, originally from the Lebanon, first settled on Cyprus in the 7th century; they are a Latin sect owing allegiance to the Pope and holding their services in Syriac.

On the outskirts of the village the small barrel-vaulted church of the **Panayia** stands by the road, half-sunk into the ground: the frescoes inside have been whitewashed over, but two tiny pews and a statue of the Virgin remain, and you may find fresh flowers on the little tiled altar. The centre of

Koruçam is dominated by the enormous Maronite church of **Ayios Georgios** (1940), cathedral-like in dimensions and garishly decorated within; on the other side of the road is the 15th-century convent church, lovingly maintained and set in a garden ablaze with colour. Inside there is little to see, but a nun will proudly illuminate the bulbs in the Virgin's halo for you. Koruçam appears large and quite prosperous, with some new houses, and the continued presence of the Maronites testifies to Turkish tolerance: but the people are mainly elderly. The young tend to leave for the south in quest of employment and a more familiar culture, and the long-term future of the village must be doubtful. From a ridge above the village there are extensive views of cornfields stretching all the way to the sea.

Leaving Koruçam the road skirts the plain, descending gently past a military area (photography forbidden); approaching Tepebaşı you are forced to detour to the right to avoid another military base. Rejoin the route here, having bypassed Çamlıbel.

The road now winds scenically through the foothills of the mountains, a landscape of trees, gorges and small rivers, past **Geçitköy** (Panagra) and a large reservoir, before climbing once more. Three miles (5 km) further on is **Çamlıbel** (Myrtou). Here the military presence is pronounced and the town's major site, the **Monastery of Ayios Pandeleimon**, patron saint of physicians, is inaccessible to visitors although no longer in use by the army. The church is late 16th-century, but the monastery was abandoned in the 1950s and contained little of interest. Just before the monastery there is a major junction manned by a soldier: straight on is the road for Lefkoşa, but we turn right for Lefke and Güzelyurt – a sign declares that military vehicles have 'prioption' and civilians are not permitted to travel at over 30 mph, but this seems little observed. Proceed through the village (there is a petrol station), bearing left where a new road has been constructed to skirt another army base, towards **Tepebaşı**, a village enjoying a commanding position on a ridge with extensive views over the coastal plain.

A mile further on, a turning to the right leads down a good single track road through pines loud with cicadas to the village of **Akdeniz** (Ayia Irini); fossils of pigmy hippopotami have been found here. On the coast beyond is the ancient temple site of **Paleokastro**, where a hoard of some 2,000 7th–6th century BC terracotta statues varying in size from four feet to a few inches was excavated in 1929; but once again the military are here and drivers are warned with shrill whistles against approaching the shore. Various dirt tracks to the left may appear to offer alternative routes to the long sandy beach which lines this part of the coast, but unfortunately the soldiers are everywhere and it is a waste of time to attempt this at present.

Instead, pursue the main road through **Kalkanlı** (Kalokhorio), where the Sakaryalı café, set on the edge of the plateau, offers unrivalled views over Güzelyurt Bay to the Troodos Mountains beyond. From here onwards the countryside is almost entirely given over to citrus production: Asil Nadir's large Sunzest factory is prominent by the road as you approach **Güzelyurt** (Morphou). Beside the road as it enters the town stands a preserved steam locomotive, a survivor of the British-built Cyprus Government Railway which ran between Güzelyurt and Gazimağusa, via Lefkoşa: mainly used for transporting copper and asbestos to the docks at Gazimağusa, the line was closed in 1951 after running for less than fifty years. This engine, no. 3, was built in Philadelphia by the Baldwin Locomotive works in 1924 – today lizards play in its cab.

Güzelyurt is a bustling and important town of some 12,000 inhabitants and warrants a stop: bear right onto the road to Lefke and park behind the church (now used as a modelling school). Ahead of you is the small museum (open 09.00–13.30 and 16.30–18.30 in summer). The exhibits on the ground floor consist of geological specimens and some rather poorly stuffed examples of fish, animal oddities, Cypriot birds and domestic fowl. Upstairs is more interesting, though regrettably few of the exhibits give any indication of their provenance. Room 1 contains Neolithic and Mycenaean exhibits, which illustrate the development of pottery from the earliest red-on-white ware to the red lustre ware of the late Bronze Age; rooms 2 and 3 display pottery and other artefacts from the Late Cypriot (16th-century BC) site of **Toumba tou Skourou** 2 miles (3½ km) north of Güzelyurt, excavated in 1973 but now inaccessible among the citrus groves; here and at nearby Akdeniz some of the earliest known Minoan artefacts to reach Cyprus were unearthed, and exhibits include a terracotta model of a war chariot. Room 4 contains objects from the Geometric (1000–700 BC) and Archaic periods (700–475), and Room 5 Classical, Hellenistic, Roman and Byzantine items, including jewellery, pottery and statuary.

The curator of the museum will open the monastery of **Ayios Mamas** next door for you for a small additional fee. This is the town's most important monument and well worth visiting, since it is one of the few examples of an unchanged Greek Orthodox church interior you will see in the Republic. St Mamas is always depicted riding on a lion

The monastery church of Ayios Mamas, Güzelyurt

and is often called the patron saint of tax-evaders. He was a 3rd-century hermit who (since he lived in a cave) thought it unfair that he should have to pay the taxes demanded by the Byzantine duke. Arrested for his refusal, he was being taken to Nicosia when a lion sprang out in his path[1], whereupon Mamas subdued the beast with a gesture and proceeded to ride it the rest of the way. When he appeared thus mounted in the palace, the duke was so impressed that he exempted Mamas from taxation for life. His body lies in a sarcophagus which forms part of the north wall of the church. The holes bored in it by the Turks in the 16th century (they thought there must be treasure within) can still be seen: legend has it that sweat (or alternatively a healing balm) oozes period-ically through the holes.

The building itself was first a Roman temple, then a Byzantine church which was rebuilt in flamboyant Gothic style in the 15th century and again in 1725. The graffiti on the west door are interesting: they include the names of a M. Porey, who was French consul in 1738, and of a Russian who was cured by the saint in 1753. Inside, the iconostasis incorporates marble columns with Gothic capitals and some marble panels of the Venetian period, finely decorated; its carved woodwork, painted blue and gold, is late 16th-century – a good view of it can be obtained from the gallery. Marble pillars, two of them with Byzantine capitals, support the altar. The north and south doorways and the columns in the west window were part of the 15th-century church, as

[1] In fact it is fairly certain that there have never been lions in Cyprus.

were those in the nave. The interior, lit by a massive chandelier, glows with colour like a treasure house.

> If you feel the need of a swim, it is possible to reach a long sandy strip of beach from Güzelyurt by following signs to **Yayla** from near the museum and forking right onto a metalled road just before the village is reached. The beach can be found by crossing two dry streambeds and threading your way through a maze of tracks between citrus groves divided by large windbreaks of bamboo and conifers. The route is complex and impossible to describe in detail: a good sense of direction is essential, and the aim is to keep heading westwards (and avoid being driven north towards the military area). With luck, however, you should emerge from the citrus plantations onto a sandy plain, at the far side of which a gravel track runs behind an unpromising ridge of pebbles. Surprisingly, on the other side of this bank you will find a long narrow and deserted stretch of soft sand which shelves gently into the warm, shallow and crystal clear waters of Güzelyurt Bay.

Leave Morphou, following signs for Lefke between the monastery and a new concrete mosque and bearing right at the roundabout to traverse the extensive suburbs. **Aydınköy** (Prastio) has a late 18th-century barrel-vaulted church and the less interesting 19th-century monastery of St Nicholas on the outskirts; beyond it **Gaziveren** has always been a Turkish village and was the scene of a heroic defence in 1964, when a handful of inhabitants held off a superior force of Greek troops long enough for an ultimatum from Turkey to bring about their withdrawal. Shortly afterwards the broad river Doğancı is crossed and a new road sweeps through **Yeşilyurt**; just past the village, a turning to the right (signposted Cengiz Topel Hastanesı) leads to the old hospital of the Cyprus Mines Corporation, handed over the government after 1974, and the golf club (*see p. 69*). Here the sea reappears, framed by the foothills of the Troodos tumbling down to the sea in Tillyria. Passing a grim concrete monument to the dead of the Turkish Air Force, set in an arid concrete garden, you reach the once flourishing port of **Gemikonağı** (Karavostasi).

For many years the product of the important copper mines of Skouriotissa used to flow through here, but the mines now lie just beyond the Attila Line (and would anyway have been worked out by 1976). Today Gemikonağı is one of the most depressing places in North Cyprus: heaps of copper slag lie around and the jetty is sagging, while collapsing warehouses, rusting machinery and a few ancient hulks rotting on the shore complete an atmosphere of grim dereliction.

A left turn here will take you past a UNIFCYP church to **Lefke**, an attractive university town which was a principal barony in the medieval period. Encircled by citrus groves, date palms and cypress, the town has the feel of an oasis standing out from the surrounding tawny hills. Lefke has some fine old houses and two mosques (each on the site of an older church): outside one of them is a sizeable rococo tomb of about 1820 and some inscribed *cippi* (low memorial columns) from a large Hellenistic and Roman necropolis which surrounds the town. The copper in this area was an important resource for the ancients and blue-green patches on the surrounding hills attest to its presence today. On the outskirts of Lefke is a graveyard with a bitter inscription in three languages recording the deaths of unarmed Turkish civilians killed by 'Greek thugs'. A fine statue of Atatürk on a rearing stallion greets visitors to the town and another enormous effigy of him dominates a nearby hill – clearly intended to be visible across the frontier which is close here. The countryside around is tranquil enough today, but you cannot get far to the south or east of Lefke before being turned back.

The main road continues along the coast, and very soon after Gemikonağı a series of rough and ready signs direct you up a hill to the left where there is a small parking area near the ruins of **Soli**. Once one of the most prominent city-kingdoms on the island, Soli is supposed to have been founded (as Aepia) by Demophon, son of Theseus; the Greeks believed that around 600 BC King Philokypros transferred his capital to this site on the advice of the celebrated Athenian philosopher Solon, in whose honour the city was renamed. The city fell to the Persians in *c.* 498 BC, but flourished well into the 4th century AD, when its

Lefke, a dignified village which has always been Turkish

Mosaic pavements in the basilica at Soli

harbour silted up; it was finally destroyed by Arab raiders in the 7th century. Near the car parking area is a large late 4th-century basilica with some attractive mosaics featuring birds, fish and geometric patterns; a much smaller church was built within the ruins in the 12th century, remains of which can be seen in the eastern section. Beside it, up a stepped path, is the Roman theatre with seating for some 3,500, excavated and somewhat over-efficiently restored by a Swedish expedition in the 1930s. Looking west and seawards from the theatre the faint traces of the agora and three temples (of Isis, Aphrodite and Serapis) which were excavated by the same expedition can be discerned, though they have since been ploughed over: a well-known 1st-century BC marble statue of Aphrodite from here is in the Cyprus Museum. Excavations continued in later years, but no further work has taken place since 1974. Much of the stone from the city was plundered in the late 19th century to be used for building the quays at Port Said and the Suez Canal.

Continuing on the coast road, the road passes a small pebbly beach area with water sports facilities used by UN forces before climbing through rugged terrain past a picturesquely sited but vandalized church. After some 3½ miles (6 km), turn right on the crest of a hill onto a narrow road which winds around the hill, rising sheer from the sea, on which stands the palace of **Vouni**, with magnificent views across Güzelyurt Bay. The palace enjoys a spectacularly commanding position, and appears to have been built in the 5th century BC, probably by a puppet ruler of the Persians interested in ensuring the loyalty of pro-Greek Soli nearby. The design is essentially Oriental and suggests a lifestyle of great wealth and luxury, reflected in the sculpture, coins and gold jewellery, much of it Persian, which have been found here. The complex seems to have been destroyed by fire *c.* 380 BC, when the Persians regained control after being ousted by the Greeks, so it can only have existed for about a century.

The palace consists of a main hall (*megaron*), entered from the south-west and surrounded by apartments; from it steps lead down to a peristyle courtyard where a stone stele stands which would have supported a windlass for lifting water from the cistern below. To the east is another large courtyard surrounded by storerooms, built later when pro-Greek rulers had taken over the palace: further rainwater cisterns lie under it with channels communicating with the major rooms, part of a sophisticated plumbing system predating that of Roman Salamis, for example, by five hundred years. To the north-east is an early example of a bathhouse with a vaulted furnace below. The kitchen area lies to the right of the entrance, while to the left of the *megaron* are living quarters, further storerooms and a later entrance at the northern corner of the site. South of the palace are the remains of a **Temple to Athena**, where many votive offerings were excavated in the 1920s, and three bronze sculptures. The great appeal of Vouni, however, is perhaps not the ruins as much as the beauty of the site, which is usually deserted and offers unrivalled opportunities for contemplation of the magnificent views.

Rejoining the main road at the bottom of the hill it is possible to proceed a little further westwards, to

Yeşilırmak (Limnitis), lying in a fertile valley. Just past the village a sign to the right points to a pleasantly peaceful little beach of sand and shingle with a bar/restaurant, Basmali plaj. Beyond this, troops will turn you back, for the Attila Line is only a couple of miles away. Beyond *that*, however, and a few miles of Greek territory, lies another small piece of North Cyprus which cannot be visited – the unhappy enclave of **Erenköy** (Kokkina). This fiercely Turkish stronghold was attacked by 3,000 Greeks under General Grivas in August 1964, bringing Greece and Turkey to the brink of war and probably making the eventual split inevitable. Thereafter the Turks of Erenköy, plus the student volunteers (including a young Mr Denktaş) who had come to support them, were cut off from the rest of the mainland, and in 1974 it was a matter of pride that the village should remain Turkish territory despite its position just beyond the Attila Line. Only troops live there today, determinedly maintaining this foothold out of respect for its brave resistance: the original villagers have all been evacuated to Yenierenköy (New Erenköy) on the Kirpaşa peninsula (*see p. 153*).

The return journey to Girne provides views of the southern side of the Beşparmak mountains for much of the way. It is important to remember to turn left just before Güzelyurt or you will find yourself on a UN road to Aşağı Bostancı which leads straight towards the border.

LEFKOŞA (NICOSIA)

Lefkoşa is probably built on the site of the ancient city of Ledroi, which is known to have been ruled by Lefkos, son of Ptolemy Soter, in 280 BC (whence the names by which Cypriots have always referred to their capital). The city grew in the early Byzantine period, when Arab raids on the more important coastal settlements increasingly drove the inhabitants to seek refuge inland, and following the destruction of Constantia (Salamis) became the *de facto* capital, a role reinforced by the Lusignans who called the city Nicosie. We find it referred to as Cossia in 1211, when it had 'inhabitants without number, all very rich', and certainly the 12th to 15th centuries saw the city's greatest prosperity: palaces, churches and monasteries proliferated in a golden age only ended by the invasion of the Mamelukes from Egypt in 1426, when Nicosia was sacked. In the following century the Venetians radically altered the town, reducing its circumference from seven to three miles and throwing up the massive wall, with eleven bastions, which still survives. Among the many palaces and churches they destroyed in the interests of a clear field of fire beyond the new walls was the monastery of San Domenico, the last resting place of most of the Lusignan monarchs.

When the Turks made their inevitable attack and the city fell, it is recorded that 20,000 of the inhabitants were massacred. Lefkoşa remained the capital city, but never recovered its former prosperity: in 1570 the cosmopolitan population (including, we are told, Italians, French, Greeks, Maronites, Armenians, Copts, Abyssinians, Syrians and Georgians) numbered about 50,000. Three hundred years later, when the British arrived in 1878, the city was largely derelict and numbered a mere 11,500 souls. Today the northern sector retains a provincial feel: mouldering buildings of great age and elegance stand cheek by jowl with unlovely modern structures, litter blows around vacant lots and there is a general sense that time has stood still.

The route from Girne heads for the pass over the mountains below St Hilarion, then descends to cut straight as a lance across the Mesarya plain. The surrounding landscape is dull and, in summer, an unrelieved parched brown, though tree-planting along the road may one day

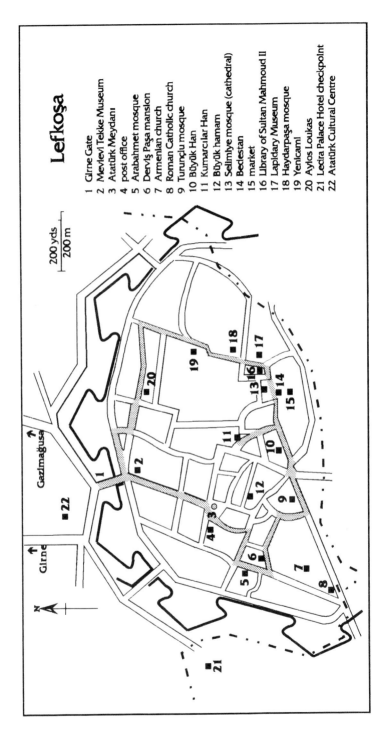

Lefkoşa

1 Girne Gate
2 Mevlevi Tekke Museum
3 Atatürk Meydanı
4 post office
5 Arabahmet mosque
6 Derviş Paşa mansion
7 Armenian church
8 Roman Catholic church
9 Turunçlu mosque
10 Büyük Han
11 Kumarcılar Han
12 Büyük hamam
13 Selimiye mosque (cathedral)
14 Bedestan
15 market
16 Library of Sultan Mahmoud II
17 Lapidary Museum
18 Haydarpaşa mosque
19 Yenicami
20 Aytos Loukas
21 Ledra Palace Hotel checkpoint
22 Atatürk Cultural Centre

200 yds
200 m

Gazimağusa

Girne

improve the outlook. The largely unattractive modern outskirts are reached through the suburban towns of Gönyeli and Ortaköy, both traditionally Turkish settlements which were the victims of terrorist violence in the years before 1974. Crossing the bypass at a large monumental roundabout the road traverses the residential districts of Kumsal to the right and Yenişehir where you should turn left at another roundabout, then right at the next T-junction to approach the north side of the walls at the Girne gate. In the broad avenue of Cemal Gürsel outside the walls are stops for buses and *dolmuşes* to other parts of the Republic, and by following the road round to the left it is usually possible to park and walk back to the gate: alternatively drive through the gate and find a space inside the old town.

The **Girne (Kyrenia) gate** was an integral part of the Venetian city walls until 1931 when the British demolished the adjoining walls to permit the flow of traffic, leaving the gate isolated in the middle of the road. A plaque above it gives 1562 as the date of its construction. There is regular talk of siting a tourist information office in the room above the gate (an Ottoman addition), but at the time of writing this has yet to happen.

Passing down Girne Caddesi, the avenue beyond, the six domes of the **Mevlevi Tekke Museum** appear almost immediately on the left. This building was the 17th-century monastery of the 'whirling dervish' sect (*derviş* means 'humble' in Turkish) founded by the mystic poet Jelal-ed-din Rumi in the 13th century and banned by the secularist Atatürk in 1925: the chief rite of the sect was an ecstatic whirling dance, setting their white robes flaring, which was performed with one palm facing down and one up to symbolise man's place as a bridge between earth and heaven. A number of finely carved pillars and gravestones lie around the courtyard, and inside the buildings an interesting and eclectic collection of Turkish Cypriot memorabilia, mostly well labelled in Turkish and English, is displayed: exhibits include photographs, examples of embroidery and calligraphy, illuminated Korans, household goods, 18th-century raised shoes for the bathroom, inlaid with mother of pearl, even a wind-up gramophone, donated by Mrs Denktaş, on which the curator plays traditional Turkish music. The main room contains the 'dance floor' where the whirling took place, with a musicians' gallery above; adjoining is a chamber containing the tombs of 16 sheikhs of the order, most of them embellished with a plaster representation of a sheikh's camel-hair hat; the oldest dates from the 17th century, the last died as recently as 1954.

Looking down on Atatürk Meydanı: the British office buildings to the left replaced a palace used by the Venetian and Turkish governors

Atatürk Meydanı (Square), in which Girne Caddesi culminates, is the hub of northern Lefkoşa. In the centre stands a granite column erected by the Venetians and once topped by the Lion of St Mark; the pillar was not unnaturally removed by the Turks, but the British reinstated it, this time surmounted with a copper globe. Venetian coats of arms, however, can still be seen around the base.

The brown stone buildings with verandahs to the right (still marked with the Lion and Unicorn emblem) are government offices, a legacy of the British colonial period. On the other side of the square is the old-established Rüstem's bookshop, and to the right the towering block of the 4-star Saray Hotel. This has a restaurant on the eighth floor, and a balcony from which a fascinating and revealing panorama of the whole city can be enjoyed: the contrast between the low-level, largely medieval buildings of the northern city and the brash but prosperous modernity of the south could not be more marked.

To tour the city systematically, bear half-right past the Sarayönü Mosque behind the Saray Hotel, down Müftü Raci Efendi Sokak (Street) and right into Müftü Ziyai Efendi Sok. Turning left at the end brings you to the **Arabahmet Mosque**, peacefully set amongst tall cypresses. The mosque, named for the builder of the Mevlevi Tekke, has a large Byzantine-style dome on four arcaded arches and is paved with 14th-century gravestones from an earlier church: they include those of the crusader Louis de Nores (died 1369) and Francisco Cornaro, a member of the family which was to give Cyprus her last queen. Here a hair of the Prophet's beard is preserved and displayed annually to the faithful. Head south from the mosque, past some very dilapidated little shops and left into Beliğ Paşa Sok., where the **mansion of Derviş Paşa** with a projecting upper storey has been beautifully restored to give an idea of a wealthy Ottoman house in the last century: the owner founded the first Turkish newspaper on the island and the house was built in 1807. Set around a pleasant courtyard, the servants' rooms on the lower floor display household goods, a huge old loom, tools, glassware and ceramics, while upstairs are examples of sumptuously embroidered costumes. At the far end of the upper floor is a large, cool hall (*selamlık*) lined with divans with a large hookah in the centre, the epitome of Oriental luxury and elegance. (The museum is open daily during office hours.)

Directly ahead, across a patch of waste ground, stands the 14th-century **Armenian church**, formerly a Benedictine abbey but given to the Armenians by the Turks in 1570 as a reward for their assistance against the Latins; today it is inaccessible because of its proximity to the Green Line; beyond it lies a largely modern Roman Catholic church, also isolated. Heading south and east brings you through a dismal area near the Line (no photography) to what remains of Baf (Paphos) Avenue, once a principal thoroughfare. Here stands the **Turunçlu Mosque** (1845), strongly resembling a church with its buttresses and porches; the tall twin minarets of the Selimiye Mosque now appear ahead, beyond a modern shopping centre in the pedestrianized Arasta Sok., with some fashionable clothes shops. Make for them, until through an opening to the left you glimpse the massive wall of the recently restored **Büyük Han** (Great Inn). This was constructed in 1572 as a caravanserai, a centre, common in mainland Turkey, which not only offered visiting merchants accommodation and stabling for their animals, but also functioned as a warehouse and commodity market. The great door is large enough to admit a loaded camel complete with its rider, and in it is a smaller door for use when the large one is locked, known as 'the eye of the needle'. Inside there are 67 rooms arranged on two storeys around a central courtyard in which stands a small octagonal mosque with marble pillars. Along the roof the carved octagonal chimneys of the merchants' rooms below are still visible.

A little to the north, past the stubby stone minaret of the Iplik Bazari Mosque, is the much smaller **Kumarcılar**

The Kumarcılar Han was also known as the 'Han of the Itinerant Musicians'

Han (Gamblers' Inn), a late 17th-century caravanserai; the central courtyard provides a tranquil haven from the bustle of the streets outside, and one of the small rooms where the merchants slept is used by the Office of Antiquities, charged with maintaining and restoring the ancient monuments of the Republic.

From here return southwards towards the prominent minarets of the Selimiye Mosque, noting on your right an ancient **Turkish bath** (*hamam*) whose elaborate stone entrance is set some 6 feet below the present street level. The doorway formerly belonged to the 14th-century church of **St George of the Latins**, also called St George of the Poulains (Half-Castes, from the Arabic Ibn-Foulan, 'Son of Nobody', since its parishioners were mainly of mixed Frankish–Syrian descent). Inside, a nail on one of the walls marks the point to which the flood water rose when the Kanlı Dere (Pedieos) river overflowed in 1330, drowning 3,000 of Nicosia's inhabitants. The baths offer massage and salt baths or simply a shave, as well as the opportunity to swelter in each of its three small and progressively hotter rooms: the warmest reaches 65°C.

The **Selimiye Mosque**, reached next, was built as the cathedral of St Sophia and renamed in honour of Sultan Selim II (the Ottoman monarch at the time of the Turkish conquest of Cyprus). It is easily the most important medieval building in the city. Construction began in 1209 and received a useful boost in 1248 when (St) Louis IX of France arrived on the island en route to the Crusades, bringing with him a retinue of skilled French architects and engineers. Finally consecrated in 1326, the cathedral's full glory lasted less than fifty years before it was sacked by the Genoese; later the Mamelukes sacked it again and earthquakes caused further damage. The building was converted into a mosque within a week of the Turkish conquest of the city in 1570; the stained glass, gravestones and interior ornamentation were stripped out in accordance with the Islamic ban on depictions of the human form and two lofty minarets added.

Despite these incongruous appendages, however, the building remains recognisably French. Its chief glory is the west front with three decorative doorways in the large porch, each of a different design, and a great window with elaborate tracery. Inside (shoes should be removed and silence observed if prayers are in progress), the walls have been comprehensively whitewashed and the distortion enforced by the mosque's reorientation towards Mecca is at first confusing, but despite the gaudy modern carpets and the plaster of Paris tracery in the windows the elegant proportions of the building are apparent. Thick pillars with Byzantine capitals divide the nave from the two aisles, which end at an apse containing four columns removed from Salamis. The *mihrab*, facing Mecca, is in the south transept, which was the Lady Chapel (founded by Hugues III in 1270). Opposite the north door is a remaining fragment that was the archbishop's palace.

To the south of the mosque is northern Lefkoşa's large covered market, which has a lively atmosphere early in the day: it is a good place to purchase fruit and vegetables, though goods of all kinds are on sale. In front of it is the **Bedestan** (covered market), an architectural mixture, consisting essentially of two churches side by side of which the western halves have been destroyed. The building was briefly the Orthodox cathedral, but used by the Turks as a cloth market and later a grain store. Over the door through which you enter is a sculptured frieze of coats of arms, and inside some enormous vaulted arches remain, with shields on some of the capitals of the pillars, but most of the building is ruined. Two small adjoining chambers house a jumbled collection of gravestones etc. There is a small charge for entrance to the Bedestan, but for this the attendant will also admit you to the domed **Library of Sultan Mahmoud II**, in an elegant octagonal building with flying buttresses erected in 1829. The inside, decorated with a beautiful calligraphic frieze in blue and gold, contains about 1,700 books, some 700 years old; showcases display some of the more interesting volumes. He will also take you to the **Lapidary Museum** (once known as Jeffries' Museum), a charming 15th-century house containing a mixed collection of sarcophagi, columns, shields, steles and architectural features, most noticeably a flamboyant Gothic window rescued from the Lusignan palace which once stood near Atatürk Square. (If you find the Bedestan locked it may mean that the attendant is showing someone round one of the two other buildings.)

Emerging from the Lapidary Museum, the minaret of the **Haydarpaşa Mosque** looms to the north, reached up Kirlizade Sok. Originally the church of St Catherine, this 14th-century building is the second most important Gothic

This flamboyant window in the Lapidary Museum is all that remains of the royal palace of the Lusignan kings

monument in Lefkoşa after St Sophia's Cathedral. The exterior is adorned with elegant buttresses between the narrow windows and small gargoyles around the roof: the western façade is a fine example of the 'flamboyant' Gothic style, while the southern doorway is rather heavier. Inside, several carved heads have survived on the corbels of the vaulted sacristy to the north: above it is a tall chamber which may have been a treasury. A house nearby was the home of Lord Kitchener from 1880–83, when he was working on the first survey of the island. Further north are the remains of a medieval church renamed the **Yenicami** (New Mosque) in 1571, of which only a staircase and the minaret survive. Heading back towards the northern section of the wall, the 18th-century church of **Ayios Loukas** in Alsancak Sok. is now a school; continuing north and west from it will bring you to the walls opposite the Musalla or Barbaro bastion in which is the **Museum of the National Struggle**: this exhibits weapons used by the TMT (Turkish resistance), photographs and other memorabilia of the difficult years experienced by the Turkish community prior to 1974 and of the Peace Operation which brought them to an end.

Outside the walls the Venetians ensured that little of historic interest remains. Selim II Cadd., west of the Girne Gate leads to the **Ledra Palace Hotel**, where visitors from the south can cross the Line for limited periods (but not *vice versa*). Further west, the British Council offices (and that of the Consul) will be found in the smart residential area around Mehmet Akif Cadd., set in a pleasant walled garden. The Council has a library (normally open 07.30–13.30 and 15.30–18.30 Mon–Fri, closed Weds afternoons) with a selection of English books and newspapers and runs an occasional programme of films, lectures and other events. Further north in the same street a simple suburban bungalow was the scene of the brutal murder by EOKA terrorists of the family of the Turkish Cypriot Major Ilhan in 1963; it is now the **Museum of Barbarism**, displaying chilling documentation of the atrocity.

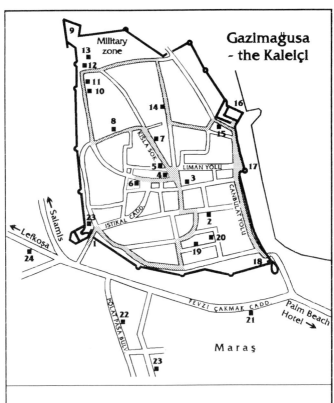

Gazimağusa – the Kaleiçi

1 Land Gate
2 St George of the Greeks
3 Lala Mustapha Paşa mosque (cathedral)
4 Venetian palace
5 St Francis' church
6 church of SS Peter and Paul
7 churches of the Knights Templar and Hospitallers
8 Nestorian church
9 Martinengo bastion
10 Ayia Anna
11 Tanner's mosque
12 St Mary of Carmel
13 Armenian church
14 Biddulph gate
15 St George of the Latins
16 Citadel (Othello Tower)
17 Sea Gate
18 Djamboulat bastion
19 Ayia Zoni
20 Ayios Nikolaos
21 tourist office
22 hospital
23 post offices
24 bus station

GAZIMAĞUSA (FAMAGUSTA)

Gazi Mağusa, the Turks' name for Famagusta, means 'unconquered Magusa', and indeed from their point of view it never has been, at least since 1571, when they were the conquerors. The city (then known as Ammochostos, literally 'hidden by the sand') was originally founded by Ptolemy Philadelphus of Egypt in the 3rd century BC and despite the influx of refugees which followed the abandonment of Salamis in 648 AD remained an obscure and unimportant village for many centuries: a visitor in 1211 referred to it as 'slightly fortified'. Famagusta's mushroom growth really began after the fall of Acre in 1291, when Henri II invited Christian refugees from the Holy Land to seek asylum there. The wealth and expertise of the resulting new settlers gave the city a major boost and it grew rapidly, soon becoming one of the most important and wealthy cities in the Levant. All the religions of the Near East built churches and convents here (it was said there was a church in Famagusta for every day of the year), and all the major nations of the Mediterranean felt it necessary to establish trading houses to claim a share of the wealth of the East which flowed through the city. The nobility and the merchant class alike were famous worldwide for their affluence, frequently employing over two hundred servants apiece. 'I dare not speak of their precious stones and golden tissues and other riches', wrote a gaping visitor in 1350, 'for it were a thing unheard of and incredible'.

But Famagusta's golden age was short-lived. In 1372, following an absurdly trivial dispute between the representatives of Genoa and Venice at the coronation of Pierre II, riots broke out which culminated in the Genoese invading the island and seizing Famagusta. They held it until 1464, and, isolated from the rest of Cyprus and deserted by its glittering population (who, like the Lusignans themselves, mostly moved to Nicosia), the city's fortunes declined. The Venetian takeover in 1489 brought a temporary improvement, for they made this now half-empty city their capital, but as we have seen (*pp. 58–9*) their concerns were purely military. The Venetians did, however, reconstruct the citadel and throw up the massive walls and bastions which still ring the old town today. But even these were unable to prevent the city falling to the Turks in 1571 after a 10-month siege famed throughout Christendom for the ferocity and heroism displayed by both sides (see p. 58). During the Turks' unrelenting bombardment it is said that 100,000 cannonballs fell on the town and scarcely a building in it was left intact.

Famagusta became Turkish and the walled city (the Kaleiçi) has remained so ever since. But beyond repairing the walls the Turks built nothing new within them, using the city as a prison for dissidents and others who had offended the Sultan of the day: in 1843 it had only 'a miserable population of 500 Turks', but the British Consular Agent who made this report noted that 'Famagusta could readily be rendered strong and impregnable by a European Power', and that there were still some 300 churches. Shortly after this, however, further damage was inflicted on the town when large quantities of stone were removed by the British to build the quays of Port Said and the Suez Canal: it is related that whole churches were torn down for this mundane purpose.

July 1974 saw a second siege of Gazimağusa, though this one lasted only three weeks. When news came of the landings at Karaoğlanoğlu, the Greek National Guard attacked Turkish Cypriots living outside the walls of Gazimağusa; many were able to escape through secret passages into the Kaleiçi, and 11,000 were besieged until the Turkish troops were able to reach the city with supplies.

Since the sixteenth century, the Greek population of Famagusta had lived outside the walls, in the Maraş (known to the Greeks as Varosha, though this is itself a Turkish word meaning suburb). Prior to 1974 the Maraş had grown into a thriving port and the island's biggest resort, its Greek population of some 40,000 swollen by many thousands more in the tourist season. The long golden beach was lined with some forty hotels and a similar number of apartment blocks. Today the hotels and luxurious villas of the Maraş are crumbling silently behind barbed wire; weeds grow in its streets and sea water has corroded its water pipes beyond repair. The Turkish army stopped short of advancing so as to incorporate the area into North Cyprus and it is now a ghost town in no man's land, an eerie and macabre monument to the wasteful disruption caused by intercommunal conflict. A single UN observation post occupies the largest hotel, its lonely lights shining forlornly at night. To the south and west lie the UN buffer zone and the British Sovereign base at Dhekelia.

Approaching Gazimağusa from the capital, the road passes unexceptional suburbs and the main bus station to reach a roundabout embellished with a startling bronze statue showing Atatürk with figures crawling all over his body. Here the visitor gets his first sight of the city walls and the huge Land Gate which was the main entrance to the town in the Middle Ages. Nowadays the town is entered by a modern bridge over the fosse beside the gate. Once within the walls, the simplest plan if you are driving is probably to turn sharp right, following the walls, and head left into the town centre at the second or third opportunity; you should then be able to see **St Nicholas' Cathedral** ahead of you, and near at hand the lofty ruins of the church of **St George of the Greeks**, in front of which it is possible to park in the shade (in the morning). Only three walls of this church survive, but there are traces of tombs in the walls with fragments of 15th-century painting visible in the apses; huddling next to it is the original Byzantine cathedral of **Ayios Symeon**, with fragments of painting and two apses. Once domed with a columned nave, it was badly damaged by the Turkish cannons in 1571 and never reconstructed.

The old town of Famagusta is bewildering at first; much of it resembles a bomb site (which is precisely what it is), with the ruined walls and towers of numerous churches rising above the horizon here and there, amid large tracts of empty desolation. Parking is relatively easy, for the town has never expanded to fill the space available within its walls since large portions of it were to all practical purposes destroyed. The shopping centre, though small, is however a lively and good-humoured place, with an excitingly oriental feel, and the experience of wandering around this strangely beautiful city is unique and memorable.

From St George of the Greeks head towards the Lusignans' cathedral, noting the 16th-century barrel-vaulted church of the Holy Cross, now the **Sinan Paşa Mosque**, to your left. The cathedral of St Nicholas, now the **Lala Mustafa Paşa Mosque**, is the most important monument of old Famagusta, a magnificent example of 14th-century Gothic architecture with a strong resemblance to the cathedral at Rheims (though the risk of earthquakes compelled Gothic buildings in Cyprus to be less lofty than their European counterparts). Consecrated in 1326, it was here that the Lusignan kings came to be symbolically crowned as kings of Jerusalem after their coronation as kings of Cyprus in Nicosia, and here Jacques II and his infant son Jacques III, the last sovereigns of the line, are buried. The western façade has three large porches, with straight-gabled canopies above, elaborately carved, and a splendid window of six lights in the centre, surmounted by a rose window. The twin towers were destroyed by the Turkish bombardment.

St Nicholas Cathedral (Lala Mustafa Paşa Mosque)

Inside, the usual coat of whitewash covers the walls, the altars and tombs have been cleared away and the stained glass replaced with tracery in plaster of Paris; the purity of the design and the uncluttered architectural outlines are the easier to appreciate as a result. Two rows of solid round columns support the vaulting over the nave and the two aisles and there are fine lancet and rosette windows in the triple apse. A few medieval tombs remain exposed to view in the north aisle.

Outside stands a great *ficus sycomoros* tree with fig-like fruits; it may be as old as the cathedral itself. A later building, once perhaps the sacristy but now housing a bank, projects from the north wall. The small domed structure nearby was used as a Koranic school. At the other end of the *parvis*, or forecourt, stands a 16th-century vaulted extension, once two storeys, with a finely decorated arched doorway and two circular windows surmounted by Venetian coats of arms. Now used as a washroom by worshippers at the mosque, it contains a 20-foot section of a marble frieze from Salamis, representing cavorting animals. A Lusignan tombstone nearby was used by the Turks as a convenient slab on which to lay out the bodies of their dead. Most sinister of the monuments to be seen in the *parvis* are the two pillars of grey granite (also doubtless from Salamis) between which the gallant Marc Antonio Bragadino was flayed to death after surrendering the city to the Turks (*see p. 58*).

Weaving through the traffic in the dusty, down-at-heel square outside the cathedral, it is hard to imagine this was the heart of one of the wealthiest cities on earth, and later the parade ground of Venetian power; but on the other side of the square still stands the façade of the Venetian *provveditore's* palace, with three arches supported by columns (again removed from Salamis), the central arch bearing the arms of Giovanni Renier, Governor of Cyprus in 1552 when it was built. The courtyard beyond is now used for parking; on the left is the cell in which the Ottoman poet Namık Kemal, 'the Shakespeare of Turkey', was imprisoned for three years as punishment for writing a play judged seditious by the Sultan. To the right stand the remains of the monastery **Church of St Francis** with a disused Turkish bath built around the apse: it now houses the Old Town disco. To the south-west is the stocky **Church of St Peter and Paul**, now the public library. This church, well-preserved in consequence of its having been converted to use as a mosque, is said to have been built with the profits of a single trading expedition in 1360 during the reign of Pierre I: its flying buttresses are less than elegant, but the Gothic north door is impressive even though the coats of arms which once surrounded it have been erased. From it Istiklâl Caddesi, a street in which most of the old town's restaurants and shops (predominantly jewellers) can be found, leads back to the Land Gate.

North of the cathedral is the city's covered market and an area where old men sit around and a colourful shoeblack plies his trade. Walking north west from St Francis' along Kişla Sok., once lined with the luxurious houses of the Lusignan nobility, brings you to the twin churches of the **Knights Templar and the Hospitallers**, ironically close neighbours in view of the Orders' traditional rivalry. Both are small 14th-century structures, the Templars' (the larger) with sockets for flagstaffs on the gables and the Order's arms on a marble lintel. Turn left at the next opportunity to reach the **Nestorian church**, built by Sir Francis Lakhas, a great merchant prince, in 1359. Nestorians (also sometimes called Chaldeans, after the language used in their rite) were a Christian sect from Syria, whose tradition has been inherited by the Assyrians of Iraq and Iran. This triple-apsed building has been used as a camel stable in its time but was in use as an Orthodox church as recently as 1963; today it is a cultural centre for the University of the Eastern Mediterranean and usually locked. It used to be known to the Greeks as 'St George the Exiler', from the legend that if dust from its floor was left in an enemy's house, he would die or leave the island within a year. Rising to the north-west can be seen the roofless church of **Ayia Anna**, said to contain murals – a tall yet strangely squat and graceless building with a broad belfry. Beyond it stand the so-called '**Tanner's Mosque**', originally a 16th-century church, the shell of **St Mary of Carmel** and the smaller 14th-century **Armenian Church**, both of which once had monasteries attached: the latter resembles several other vaulted Cypriot churches in containing earthenware jars built into the ceiling to improve the acoustics. Unfortunately all these churches lie within the confines of a military camp, so there is no access to them and photography is forbidden.

The camp extends as far as the massive **Martinengo bastion**, jutting like a spearhead at the north-west corner of the walls. An impressive monument to the great age of military fortification, the bastion was built by Giovanni Girolamo Sanmichele in the 1550s; complete with side cannon ports and vents for gunsmoke in its 20-foot thick walls, the bastion commands an area of at least a square mile, and the Turks left it well alone during the siege.

Walking seawards from the camp, turn inland again along Naim Efendi Yolu before reaching the sea wall to head towards the cathedral once more. To your right are some decayed early 18th-century bath houses, and on the left ruins thought to be those of St Clare's convent. A little further along on the right is the **Biddulph gate**, an elaborate doorway named after a British High Commissioner whose efforts saved it from demolition. After this, head left towards the sea wall past the lofty and picturesque ruins of **St George of the Latins**, built in the French style in the late 13th century; once fortified and therefore presumably built before any walls encircled the city, little survives of the church save the north wall, choir and the vaulted sacristy, with pillars and a single gargoyle. On the capitals, carved grape clusters can be made out and in one case what is thought to be a line of bats.

(above and below) Bellapais Abbey: Gothic splendour with a mountain backdrop (bottom) The magnificent mosaic floors of the Ayias Trias basilica, near Sipahi

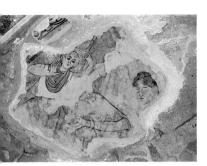

Fresco at Salamis   (right) Mosaic at Soli   (below) The
colours of this fresco still glow in the Antiphonitis monastery
church, Esentepe

Nearby stands the '**Othello Tower**', the moated Lusignan citadel built to protect the harbour and reconstructed for artillery by the Venetians in 1492. The name may derive from Cristoforo Moro, who was the Venetian Lieutenant-Governor from 1505–8 (and apparently returned to Venice without his wife), but Shakespeare's play simply mentions 'a seaport in Cyprus' and there is no evidence that it was based on a historical occurrence. The entrance is surmounted by a Venetian lion and an inscription recording the prefecture of Niccolo Foscarini, under whom the remodelling of the citadel was begun. The Venetians reduced the four square Lusignan towers to the level of the battlements and made them round to withstand gunfire; they also strengthened the walls and removed the upper levels of the citadel. A model showing different stages in the evolution of the structure can be viewed in the custodian's lodge. Inside is a courtyard surrounded by vaulted chambers and a large 14th-century refectory building, 92 ft (28 m) long with five vaulted bays, showing the arms of Jerusalem on the keystones. Within the walls are long passageways with lofty ventilation shafts up to 23 ft (7 m) high; the Venetians filled many of these with rubble or simply sealed them up when they were reinforcing the walls and the intriguing possibility remains that somewhere within the 30-foot thick walls there may still be a cache of treasure to be found. Cannon balls and old cannon lie around and steps lead to the upper sections of the citadel, where there is a good view of the harbour (no photography) from a large platform over the

The Lion of St Mark protects the entrance to the Citadel

vault with the remains of triple pillars set in the walls. The Othello Tower is open 09.00–17.00 daily for a small charge.

From the Tower continue along the sea wall down Canbulat Yolu; on the corner with Liman Yolu is Petek's Pastaneleri, a café and sweetmeats shop displaying a mouthwatering selection of honeyed confections and well worth a visit. By the Sea Gate opposite stand two stone Venetian lions. At the south-eastern corner, past an area of almost total dereliction where stunted sunflowers are cultivated, lies the Venetian Arsenal or **Djamboulat bastion**; here in 1570 the Turkish hero Canbulat Bey destroyed a fiendish Venetian weapon consisting of a wheel covered with knives which protected the entrance by running his horse onto the spikes; his tomb is within the bastion with a small museum which displays plans of the 1974 siege of Gazimağusa as well as items of historic interest and Turkish Cypriot culture (open 09.00–13.30, 16.30–18.30 in summer).

Return up the inside of the walls past a memorial commemorating the Turks who died in Gazimağusa in July 1974, and turn back towards the centre and your car, noting the ruined, domed church of **Ayios Nikolaos** (once covered with frescoes) and further west the pretty little cruciform church of **Ayia Zoni**, a sturdy and well-preserved 14th-century building with traces of frescoes visible within. Alternatively continue along the walls to inspect the **Land Gate**, known to the Turks as the *Akkule* ('white flag'), because it was here that the Venetians raised their flag of surrender. A 30-foot high arch frames the original gate and within the Rivettina Bastion to the west is a complex of rooms with gun ports and dungeons, some of them bedded into natural outcrops of rock; a cannon ramp leads to the top, from which there are good views of the city.

Drive back and leave the Kaleiçi through the Canbulat Gate. A road to the left leads to the luxury Palm Beach hotel and the northern limit of the Maraş: from the terrace and beach of the Palm Beach the abandoned hotels stretch southwards almost as far as the eye can see. Back outside the walls the perimeter road passes a small tourist information office upstairs at 5 Fevzi Çakmak Cadd., and reaches a junction with Polat Paşa Bulvarı to the left, the main street which now forms the eastern edge of the Turkish new town. Here are the main civic buildings (including the Post Office) and by the road is preserved engine no. 1 of the Cyprus Government Railway: another can be seen at Güzelyurt, the other terminus of this short-lived line. Further south the boulevard is deflected by the need to skirt the Maraş: fine arcades, overgrown gardens and ruined mansions can be glimpsed beyond the barrier and, at least one church, as this

The Maraş, seen from the Palm Beach: soon these buildings will have stood empty for 20 years

once prosperous quarter sinks every year further towards total disintegration; but it is forbidden to stop or take photographs.

Driving once more around the outside of the walls their full extent is apparent. Their average height is 50 ft (15 m) and parts are up to 27 ft (8 m) thick, while the surrounding fosse has in some places been excavated out of solid rock. There were twelve powerful bastions, of which the **Martinengo bastion** at the north-west corner was almost a castle in itself. It contains ventilation shafts through which the smoke of the cannon could escape, and several tunnels and hidden chambers; on the eastern side a 'cavalier' or large gun platform, while projecting 'flankers' enabled gunfire to be directed backwards along the walls. Wisely the Turks made no attempt to attack it in 1571.

Environs of Gazimağusa

The road north from the Martinengo bastion passes rapidly through the city's northern suburbs. At the first roundabout heading north there is a taxi rank. Another roundabout is traversed and the city's northern suburbs quickly disappear. About $3\frac{1}{2}$ miles ($5\frac{1}{2}$ km) out from this roundabout, by the Golden Terrace restaurant, a track leads to **Glapsides Beach**, a popular bathing place with clean, soft sand, shallow water and a beach bar. A mile further on, another stretch of pleasant beach is reached down a once-metalled dirt track: this is **Silver Beach**, a long stretch of gently shelving sand which gets deep very slowly – excellent for families with young children. This beach lies at the southern extremity of the Salamis ruins and swimmers may explore the harbour of the ancient city from here. The northern entrance to the ruins is about a mile further north, signposted off the main road.

Salamis

Salamis was for many centuries the leading city of ancient Cyprus and its ruins are the most important archaeological site on the island. According to legend the city was founded by the Homeric hero Teucer when he was exiled by his father Telamon, king of the Greek island of Salamis, on his return from the Trojan war in *c.* 1180 BC; doubtless the simultaneous decline of nearby Enkomi (*see pp. 146–8*) was not unrelated. The city prospered as trade with the outside world developed, benefiting from its coastal position opposite the Near East. By the 8th century it was a major trading centre and though tablets have been found which show that Salamis was compelled to pay tribute to the Assyrian king a hundred years later, it remained an independent Greek city-state and *c.* 560 became the first city on Cyprus to mint its own coinage, under King Evelthon, whom Herodotos mentions. The following century the city fell to the Persians, who installed puppet rulers and remained in control until their defeat by Alexander the Great almost 200 years later: only under the visionary King Evagoras, who ousted the pro-Persian ruler of Salamis in 411 and came close to uniting the whole island against the foreign oppressor, was there a brief interlude of independence, ended when Evagoras was murdered in 374. The upheavals following Alexander's death saw Salamis under siege and the suicide of the last of the royal line, King Nicocreon, in 295 BC. But the Hellenistic and Roman periods which followed brought a resurgence of prosperity, especially from shipbuilding and foreign trade, despite the Romans' preference for Paphos as their capital and severe earthquakes in 76–7 AD. The city was an early centre of Christianity; it was also the home of a large Jewish community until their expulsion after the massacre of 117 AD (*see p. 52*). Under the Byzantines Salamis once again became the capital of Cyprus, but its glory was shattered by a disastrous earthquake and tidal wave in 342. Following this the city was virtually rebuilt and renamed Constantia in honour of Constantius II, the reigning Byzantine emperor – it is largely the ruins of this city that we see today. But it never fully recovered its former pre-eminence. The harbour began to silt up and the city was finally abandoned after its sack by Arab raiders between

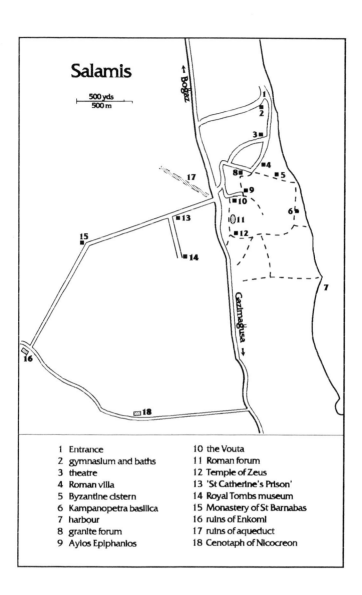

Salamis

500 yds
500 m

Boğaz →

Gazimağusa →

1 Entrance
2 gymnasium and baths
3 theatre
4 Roman villa
5 Byzantine cistern
6 Kampanopetra basilica
7 harbour
8 granite forum
9 Ayios Epiphanios
10 the Vouta
11 Roman forum
12 Temple of Zeus
13 'St Catherine's Prison'
14 Royal Tombs museum
15 Monastery of St Barnabas
16 ruins of Enkomi
17 ruins of aqueduct
18 Cenotaph of Nicocreon

647–9, its population moving south to Ammochostos (Famagusta).

The site has been plundered for building material over the centuries, notably for the building of Famagusta, but columns and other architectural features from the town can be seen all over this corner of the island. Nevertheless much of the city slept under a thick cover of sand, as it still does; the site was not systematically excavated until around 1880, and digging ceased altogether in 1974. Thus most of the city remains unexplored and there can be no doubt whatever that many more archaeological discoveries wait beneath the scrub.

The Salamis ruins are open daily from 08.00–20.00. Visitors with a serious interest in archaeology will want to spend many hours at this important site, while the more casual can visit the gymnasium, baths and theatre in an hour or two. The excavations extend over a large area, much of it covered with thick undergrowth. Stout shoes, long socks and some form of head-covering are strongly recommended if you are going to explore them seriously. In summer it is sensible to avoid the hottest part of the day by starting your visit early in the morning or after 15.00. There is access to a narrow beach from the ruins, however, so a visit can be combined with a cooling swim. Nowadays the usual entrance is from the north, signposted from the main Gazimağusa-Boğaz road about 5 miles (8 km) north of Gazimağusa. Here there is parking by the sea and a restaurant; alternatively it is possible to drive into the site and park near the theatre.

The **gymnasium and baths** at the northern end of the site date from the 4th century AD, when they were reconstructed following the destruction of their Hellenistic and Roman predecessors in the great earthquakes of 332 and 342 AD. Excavated between 1952 and 1955, the gymnasium would in classical times have been a *palaestra* or exercise ground for the athletes of the city, adjoining the baths. Around the court are stoas composed of marble columns which were all toppled by earthquakes and re-erected in the 1950s; neither they nor their capitals match each other – the Byzantine rebuilders probably took them from the nearby theatre and amphitheatre. The main entrance was through a triple portico to the south where an inscribed dedication to Ptolemy V Epiphanes (203–181 BC) can be seen between two of the columns. At the south-west corner was a semi-circular open plan latrine with seating for 44: traces of the impressive plumbing arrangements are still visible. The eastern stoa adjoining the baths has fluted columns larger than the others and is paved with *opus sectile*, the small

Salamis, the eastern stoa of the gymnasium

geometrically arranged squares of coloured marble pre-
ferred by the Christian Byzantines to the mosaic scenes
favoured by their pagan predecessors. An altar to Hermes
once stood here; it is now inaccessible to all in the
Famagusta museum, which is within the Maraş. At each
end of the stoa is a rectangular swimming pool and around
the north one stand some of the Roman statues which
originally adorned the gymnasium, including a figure of
Persephone (lacking hands or face) in dark marble: most of
the statues were removed to the Cyprus Museum in
southern Lefkoşa.

The lofty façade of the baths themselves is Byzantine.
Inside is a rectangular *tepidarium* with an octagonal cold
pool (or *frigidarium*) at each end. Part of the floor has been
left unrestored to show the hypocaust below, in which brick
pillars supported the floor to permit the flow of hot air
beneath. In the semi-dome above a recess in the south wall
part of a fresco dating from the 3rd century can be seen. To
the east is the main hall, containing the hot pool, with
sudatoria (sweating rooms) on each side: these have heating
ducts in the floor and vaulted recesses which may have
contained individual baths. Both the main hall and the
northern *sudatorium* terminate in apses. In niches in the
southern hall there are small patches of mosaic, one
probably depicting Artemis and Apollo slaying the children
of Niobe and the other the river god Eurotas with Zeus
portrayed as a swan: in the northern one there is a mosaic
picture of some oranges. Near the buttresses which support
the northern wall of the complex was the *praefurnium*

(furnace room), where slaves supplying the heat to the hypocaust system doubtless sweated as freely as their masters above.

Heading south, past steps and a ruined arched building adjoining the baths, the path passes an amphitheatre (not yet excavated) to reach the partially restored **Roman theatre**, built in the reign of Augustus and only discovered in 1959. In Roman theatres (unlike in Greek) the action took place on a raised stage behind a proscenium decorated with statues, and remains of the high wall behind the stage survive. The semi-circular orchestra in front, some 90 ft (27.5 m) in diameter and marble-paved, had an altar to Dionysos at its centre, and 50 rows of seats could accommodate an audience of up to 15,000, making this the largest ancient theatre in Cyprus. The lower benches still show traces of the limestone with which they were dressed and there are higher seats for the civic dignitaries in the central section. The theatre was almost completely destroyed by the earthquakes of the 4th century and much of it was removed to be used in the reconstruction of the gymnasium.

To the west lie more baths, unexcavated and buried in undergrowth. Much of the site is thus covered: wild flowers proliferate, but it means that a keen eye is required to spot some of the more vestigial remains. The main path passes behind the theatre and forks left through an area where the only visible ruin is that of a **Roman villa** about 250 m along on the left; it has the remains of a spiral staircase and water conduits visible in the floor. Just past it is a crossroads: turn left here towards the sea, passing a **Byzantine underground cistern**. It contains early Christian inscriptions and some small wall paintings, but access is dangerous, requiring a ladder and lights, and the entrance is usually locked (the key may be obtained from the Department of Antiquities office in Gazimağusa, by the Namık Kemal prison). Just after the path turns right are the remains of the large **Kampanopetra basilica** (4th century): at the west end of the church was a colonnaded courtyard with a well in the centre; beyond lay the church in which the outlines of three aisles and two outer passages can be discerned – in the southern one are some marble gravestones. Another courtyard to the east provided the original entrance and here there were baths, with a fine mosaic preserved. Further on lies the **harbour**, reached past an area of ruins which may predate the Byzantine reconstruction: the harbour is now submerged and the jetty lies some way out to sea, but fragments of pottery and marble (and occasionally more significant remains) can be picked up by beachcombers with relative ease. (Anything of serious interest found should be reported to the custodian; these days the unauthorised exporter of antiquities is, quite properly, prosecuted with rigour.)

Back at the crossroads, turn left to pass (on your right) the '**granite forum**', so named for the enormous 18 ft (5.5 m) columns which can be seen lying around in the undergrowth: their pinkish tinge is a clear sign that they were brought from Aswan in Upper Egypt. To the left, the ruins of what is thought to have been a water clock are a disappointing circular heap of stones half hidden by vegetation. The path now curves sharply left towards the **basilica of Ayios Epiphanios** on the left, 100 m further on. Built as Constantia's metropolitan church between 368 and 403 by the bishop after whom it is named, this basilica is the largest known on Cyprus: it is some 190 ft (58 m) long. Its broad central nave terminates in a stepped apse and is separated by columns from two side aisles: at the end of the southern aisle can be seen the marble-lined tomb where the remains of Bishop Epiphanius lay. The Saracens wrecked the church in the 7th century, after which a smaller tripledomed church was built onto the original building, with the bishop's grave at its western end; this church is said to have been still in use as late as the 14th century.

From the basilica the road bears right, past a huge 7th-century **cistern**, once vaulted (and hence known as the '*Vouta*'). An aqueduct carried water to Constantia from the perpetual spring at Değirmenlik 35 miles (56 km) away, and here it was stored and distributed via a network of pottery pipes throughout the city. Adjacent is the colossal **Roman forum** (sometimes called the Stone Forum), at 750 × 180 ft (230 × 55 m) one of largest known in the Roman world. Restored under Augustus, only a single pillar now survives from the long columned porticoes which stood in front of the many shops that once doubtless lined the sides. Further south a raised mound indicates the site of the **temple of Zeus**, probably built over an earlier Hellenistic temple: looking back over the forum from this podium you can see a section of Constantia's city wall. To the south, in an almost entirely unexcavated area which is a riot of wild flowers, lay the humble quarters of the slaves and artisans who kept the city going.

Emerging from the site, turn left and note the traces of the aqueduct heading off to the north-west from opposite the southern entrance to the site. A turning inland here leads to the ancient necropolis of the city, the so-called Royal Tombs, the monastery of St Barnabas and the ruins of Enkomi, a visit to all of which can be combined with Salamis if time permits.

Royal Tombs

Almost immediately after turning onto this minor road the curved roof of Tomb 50, popularly known as 'St Catherine's Prison', appears on the left; turn left down a track immediately after it to reach the small **museum**. Here are displayed a reconstruction of one of the chariots found outside the tombs (with the original bronze attachments), the breastplates and side ornaments worn by the horses, drawings of the tombs and photographs of the excavations and of several of the articles – a throne, incense burners, decorative ivory objects, etc. – found within them. (The originals are all in the Cyprus Museum in southern Lefkoşa.)

The curator, Halid, will then take you to view a small selection of the more significant of the 150-odd tombs that have been excavated; he speaks enough English to make the tour extremely interesting. The nearest tomb (**no. 47**) has a broad, shallow *dromos* (the sloping ramp leading to the funerary chamber), in which the skeletons of two horses are gruesomely exposed – sacrificed after pulling the king's bier to be cremated at the entrance to his tomb. At the end of the *dromos* a porch of massive stone blocks forms the entrance (*propylaeum*) to the subterranean burial chamber. These tombs, all dating from the 8th and 7th centuries BC, offer a vivid insight into Mycenaean burial practices, corresponding with astonishing faithfulness to Homer's descriptions of them in the *Iliad*. The kings and other noble personages were buried, not only with their horses and chariots, but also with favourite slaves, precious possessions, food, wine and other necessities to assist them in the after-life. Most of the tombs have been looted of these grave-goods, but **Tomb 79**, visited next, yielded a wooden throne inlaid with ivory, several cauldrons of carved bronze, figurines, amphorae and even dishes which had clearly contained fish and chickens. This tomb also displays the skeletons of horses (who appear to have died terrified) in the *dromos*; the remains of four chariots were found here, two of them with their horses still yoked and wearing harness incorporating bronze bits and decorated breastplates. The chamber beyond has ledges on which sarcophagi may have been placed in later ages.

Tomb 50, nearby, presumably gained its association with the early martyr St Catherine (she of the wheel) because it was converted into a chapel dedicated to her in a later era – indeed it is said that it was in use for this purpose as late as 1950. The structure above ground, which so puzzled visitors prior to 1962 (when this necropolis was first excavated), is a building of massive stone blocks dating from the Roman period. Only when systematic digging was undertaken was it discovered that this had been erected in the 4th century on top of a tomb dating from almost a thousand years earlier: the *propylaeum* was vaulted and turned into a room with an additional storey above, the remains of which can be seen around the walls. Here also yoked horse skeletons lie in the *dromos*.

Further tombs can be visited on the other side of the track leading to the museum. The first tomb excavated (**Tomb 1**) has a fine marble frontage: it yielded large quantities of pottery from mainland Greece and Crete, as well as amphorae which once contained oil and wine propped against the walls (exactly as in the account of Patroclus' funeral in the *Iliad*). **Tomb 3**, a mudbrick beehive tomb known as the 'Tomb of the King' erected within a prominent mound nearby, contained an amphora labelled 'olive oil' in the early Cypriot script: the tomb itself was purposely located off-centre to foil grave-robbers, and two war chariots closely resembling those depicted on Mycenaean vases were found in the steep *dromos*. Nearer the track, excavations of **Tomb 2** revealed two donkeys and some evidence of human sacrifice; this one has a well-preserved inner chamber. Some distance off to the south is the **Cellarka**, a complex of miniature tombs for less eminent citizens, with stepped *dromoi* and large stones which sealed the entrances. These burial chambers appear to have been in almost continuous use from *c.* 700 BC until the end of the 4th century AD.

Monastery of St Barnabas

A few hundred metres along the minor road from the Salamis ruins lies the monastery church of St Barnabas, the Salamis-born colleague of St Paul who ended his life *c.* 75 AD as a martyr in his home city (*see p. 51*). The present double-domed church dates from 1756: several capitals from Salamis are incorporated in the structure, and a green marble column, spirally fluted, which is built into the south wall may have been salvaged from the 5th-century Byzantine church which originally stood on the site. The spacious interior is largely whitewashed, with some large, rather crude 20th-century frescoes telling the story of the saint's life and the miraculous discovery of his tomb. These are the work of three brothers who, prior to 1974, made a living painting icons which they sold to visitors. The last Orthodox monks remaining in the North, they left for the Stavrovouni monastery in the south of the island only in 1977, and the friendly custodian will respectfully show you a photograph of them as well as the grave of their mother who died, aged 92, in 1947.

St Barnabas is shortly to be opened as an icon museum, housing icons from various villages in the vicinity: one of the icons already on show on the iconostasis dates from the 2nd century. The outbuildings will display amphorae and other remnants found at Salamis and Enkomi, and there are also plans for a café in the attractive gardens behind the church (containing a tree that simultaneously produces oranges, tangerines and lemons, all grafted onto the same trunk by the monks). If all goes well, the complex is set to become a tourist attraction of the sort that North Cyprus needs. The enthusiastic custodian of the building will also lend you the key to the tiny mausoleum chapel raised over the place where Bishop Anthemios' dream foretold the saint's remains would be found under a carob tree – a singularly timely revelation which was to prove a crucial moment in the history of the island, since it resulted in the Orthodox Church of Cyprus being granted the autocephalic status which it enjoys to this day (*see p. 53*). The rock-cut tomb where the body was found, a copy of St Matthew's Gospel clasped to its breast, is reached in a lower chamber. (It seems that Anthemios was somehow able to demonstrate to the Emperor Zeno that this Gospel had not only been placed there by St Mark, but was actually written in Barnabas' own hand!)

Enkomi (Alasia)

Continuing westwards past the monastery, a T-junction is reached, where a right turn shortly brings you to the ruins of the ancient city of Enkomi. Early excavations here turned up several tombs and it was thought that the site was simply a necropolis until further digging in 1934 revealed that a sizeable town had stood here in the Late Bronze Age. The earliest finds date from the early part of the 2nd millennium BC, but it seems that it was not until *c.* 1550 that the town reached its full extent, becoming an important trading centre especially through the export of copper: the Kanlı (Pedieos) river was navigable as far as Enkomi in those days and the city had a harbour. It is known that Enkomi had trading links with Ugarit (Ras Shamra) in Syria, and tablets found at Tell el-Amarna in Egypt record tribute paid in copper to the 18th-dynasty pharoahs Amenhotep III and Akhenaten by the king of 'Alasia', a name which it is thought referred either to Cyprus in general or this city in particular. This suggests that Enkomi may have been the capital of the island from *c.* 1600 BC, and since this idea was promulgated (in 1952), the site is often referred to as 'Alasia'. The remains give evidence of a city covering an area of almost a square mile (2½ sq. km), with a population of perhaps 15,000 who, at least from *c.* 1500 BC, enjoyed a high level of wealth and prosperity: from the 14th century onwards the influence of an Achaean influx is very apparent: much Mycenaean pottery has been found and other items unearthed from tombs include gold jewellery, cylinder seals, articles made of ivory and bronze and a clay tablet inscribed with Cypro-Minoan script and as yet undeciphered. (Some of the finds made from the earliest excavations can be seen in the British Museum.) The richest tombs so far excavated date from the 14th and 13th centuries, after the Achaeans' arrival. In the 13th/12th centuries BC the town seems to have been destroyed by fire and rebuilt on a grid plan within massive, tower-capped walls: some of the blocks used in the walls weigh up to 60 tons. The town was apparently attacked by the Sea Peoples (*see pp. 48–9*) and earthquakes and the silting up of the river eventually compelled the inhabitants to abandon it in about 1075, when they moved to the recently-founded settlement at Salamis on the coast. The ruins gradually became covered with silt from the rivers nearby. There has been no excavation here since 1974, and while it is said that artefacts from Enkomi have been known to turn up on the black market in Europe, there is doubtless much of interest still to be found, including, perhaps, the palace of the ruler.

For the casual visitor the site is confusing and not particularly rewarding, once one has marvelled at the size of the site and the modern regularity of the street plan. There is very little to be seen above ground level nor any information displayed at the site; while the guardian, a charming and friendly young man from Ürgüp on the Turkish mainland, has little knowledge about the excavations to impart and even less English. For archaeology enthusiasts, however, the ruins have much interest and give a rare insight into the development of an important Late Bronze Age community.

The 13th-century BC street plan is most clearly identifiable from the slope above the site: at least four narrow east–west streets are visible, each crossing a long central street linking the north and south gates in the wall. From the custodian's house a path leads down the hill and bears right, parallel with the road, to the fortress at the north gate, where there are remnants of the massive wall and a tower. The area around here seems to have been dominated by the copper industry: south of it lie the remains of houses, in which many items of bronze were found. West of the main street, in the centre of the area divided by the four most-revealed transverse streets, is the **Sanctuary of the Horned God**, named from the small statue discovered here, which is among the most spectacular of the finds from Enkomi: a 12th-century BC bronze statue, 21 inches (55 cm) high, of a male figure wearing a helmet from which spring two large horns (needless to say, the statue is now in the Cyprus Museum, frustratingly out of reach in the southern zone of the capital).

To the south-west of the sanctuary, the exceptionally large blocks of hewn stone used in the construction of '**Building 18**' are readily identifiable: this house, originally of two storeys, has wings and an interior courtyard. It dates from the 14th century and may have been the home of a Mycenaean prince. The street beside it leads to the west gate of the city in one direction and to an extensively excavated residential area to the east, where quantities of jewellery and other items in gold and silver were revealed, as well as a large amount of Mycenaean pottery; there was another sanctuary here, where animals were sacrificed, as evidenced by the discovery of many animal skulls and a pierced slab to which the victims were tied. South of the area (across the next transverse street) is the **House of the Pillar**, possibly another sanctuary with a roof supported by a stone pillar. Further south still is the so-called **House of the Bronzes**, site of an important find of items made of that metal. Some 160 yards (150 m) beyond it lies a surviving section of the city wall with the remains of a watch tower.

Returning to the crossroads near the monastery and driving straight on brings you to Tuzla (Engomi), where (east of the village, past the church) is the so-called **Cenotaph of Nicocreon**, the last king of Salamis who was compelled to commit suicide by Ptolemy. All that there is to see here today is a stepped stone platform, once covered with earth to form a tumulus. When excavated in 1965–6 it was found that the platform, about 150 ft (45 m) long and 30 ft (9 m) high, had been built as a funeral pyre. On its summit several gold ornaments were unearthed, some bottles of gilded clay and a number of lifesize statues with very specific facial features, suggesting that they were perhaps effigies of the king's family and this was the scene of a symbolic cremation.

THE KIRPAŞA (KARPAS)

The 'panhandle' peninsula stretching towards Syria from the north-east corner of Cyprus is an area of wild beauty (there is regular talk of turning it into a National Park) and fascinating historical remains. The peninsula has been more populous and important in the past than it is today. It is littered with ancient sites, including that of the Roman city of Carpasia; and its closeness to the Levant, its water and its plentiful stocks of timber (the Kirpaşa was once entirely forested) made it an attractive landfall for seafarers from almost every civilization in the eastern Mediterranean in ancient times. Prior to 1974 it was most famous for the large-scale annual pilgrimage to the monastery of Apostolos Andreas at its tip (*see pp. 155–6*). Today, however, the pilgrims no longer come and the Kirpaşa is under-populated, tranquil and little visited; there is scarcely any traffic on the roads, no touristic development as yet, and (best of all) very little evidence of the Turkish army apart from the camp west of Yeşilköy and a small detachment near the monastery. The main hazard of a tour of the area is the friendliness of the inhabitants, who will want to detain you for hospitality and conversation, making it even harder to see all that the Kirpaşa has to offer and still get home before dark!

The reason the peninsula lacks visitors is largely due to the shortage of tourist accommodation: the roads are mostly good, but nevertheless at least two leisurely days are needed to do the area justice, which means that only the most cursory exploration is possible for most visitors based in the Girne or Gazimağusa areas. A visit to the Kirpaşa is strongly recommended, however, and holidaymakers capti-vated by the region do have the possibility of staying a night or two in one of a handful of *pansiyons* on the peninsula or, failing that, in Boğaz.

The Kirpaşa can be reached from Girne by following the coast road eastwards (*see p. 99*) and turning inland either via Kantara (*pp. 102–3*) or through Büyükkonuk. It is most easily approached from Gazimağusa, however, from which city the main road heads north past Enkomi and Salamis as described on *p. 137*. After Salamis, the road skirts the bay, passing numerous hotels and several opportunities to reach the thin strip of sandy beach that fringes the shore: Onur

Camping has a beachside restaurant, and you can buy drinks at subsidized prices at the soldier's beach of **Istanbul plaj** further to the north. A visit can also be paid to Iskele (*see p. 104*), 2 miles off the road about 5½ miles (9 km) north of Salamis.

The end of the bay is reached at the resort of **Boğaz** (Boghaz), always a Turkish village, where there are two hotels and a dozen or more restaurants, most of them specializing in fish (*see p. 23*). Approaching the village, North Cyprus' oil terminal is noticeable, but the road beyond is quiet and rural. At a crossroads 3 miles (5 km) from Boğaz a right turn leads to the terminal and cement works at **Kalecik**; a Templar castle stood by the coast in the 12th century, but scarcely a trace of it remains today. To the left is the village of **Tuzluca** (Patriki), once known for a curious local custom which required all the married men to crawl through a hole in a large stone in the churchyard each Easter Monday: any man who was unable to do this would know that this wife was unfaithful, and one villager sued for divorce on these incontrovertible grounds as recently as 1935. Beyond Tuzluca lies **Büyükkonuk** (Komi Kebir), surrounded by fertile country and small trees, from which it is possible to reach Kantara castle (*see pp. 102–3*), passing the ancient church of **Ayios Auxentios**. Six miles (9½ km) from Boğaz is **Çayırova**, with a petrol station and two churches, one converted to a mosque.

Here a turning to the right leads through **Bafra**, an unkempt village with many abandoned houses, to a broad bay of quite steeply shelving soft sand, where an uncompleted Polly Peck holiday village is quietly decaying and an evil-smelling stream peters out behind the beach: there is good swimming in this solitary spot, however, though a slight undertow and a shingle ledge make it unsuitable for small children. On the headland to the south lie the vestigial remains of the classical settlement of **Cnidos**, birthplace of the 5th-century BC doctor and historian Ctesias. If you visit the beach you can rejoin the main road up the peninsula at Pamuklu.

After the junction the road runs through a landscape of small hills, the rump of the Beşparmak range: one of them bears a patriotic inscription. A fork to the left leads to **Mehmetçik**, a traditional Turkish village. **Pamuklu**, the next settlement reached, has a large and elegant new mosque, and traces of classical columns can be seen in a crumbling stable by the road.

Soon the sea appears ahead, and 14 miles (22½ km) from Boğaz **Kumyalı** is entered. Just inside the village a metalled road to the right leads to a small fishing harbour and a strip

Denizkızı beach

The Kirpaşa coast, east of Kaplıca

The Selemiye mosque, Lefkoşa

Oranges near Güzelyurt

September sunset, Kirpaşa peninsula

of sandy beach. There is a restaurant and bar here, the Pelican Club, named for a wounded pelican blown in during the Gulf War which was operated on by Salih, the owner: with a single wing and a voracious appetite it now directs proceedings at the beach with every appearance of gratitude. Kumyalı itself is a substantial and prosperous-looking village, which was apparently larger still during the medieval period and later: it was reported as having fourteen churches in 1745. Today the principal church is that of the Archangel Michael, built in 1859, but the small church on a platform above the village is 15th-century and built over an ancient tomb: an extensive classical necropolis lies around the building. Other notable structures in the village include the small 16th-century chapel of Nikoloudhi about a mile west of the village with some frescoes remaining. The houses of Kumyalı are mostly built of the local Kirpaşa stone: the Kakozonara quarries from which it comes are nearby and provided the reason for the village's prosperity: stone for the walls of Famagusta came from here and over the entrance to the quarry is carved the date MDXXXIII. Today Kumyalı's population numbers only about 1,000, mostly families resettled from Paphos.

Three miles (5 km) further on, as the road turns inland across the peninsula, lies **Ziyamet** (Leonarisso), surrounded with vineyards, with a large church featuring ornamental plasterwork on the tower, and steps leading up to the crumbling belfry.

Here a worthwhile detour may be made by taking a turning to the right in the centre of the village (signposted for Gelincik and Kaleburnu); this leads past a small UNIFCYP post, man-

Panayia Kanakaria

ned by Australians, and after about $1\frac{1}{2}$ miles ($2\frac{1}{2}$ km) reaches the beautiful monastery church of **Panayia Kanakaria**, built in *c*. 1160, with three barrel-vaulted naves and a tall dome. The western narthex incorporates marble columns and Corinthian capitals from a still earlier church and the apse once contained a celebrated 6th-century mosaic of the Virgin and Child: however, the Cypriots believed that the coloured stones had the ability to cure skin disease and the mosaic had already suffered considerable damage before 1974 as a result; thereafter what remained was removed, to be ultimately sold in Indianapolis for almost 2 million dollars. Nowadays the church is locked. There is evidence that a large Byzantine settlement once surrounded the monastery.

If time permits, one can continue along this road through Boltaşlı, to **Derince**, with a 17th-century church: a right turn here leads past the ruins of another small church, once completely frescoed but now totally buried in a thicket of scrub, to **Taşlıca**, built on the edge of a high plateau above the coast. The ruins of a sizeable temple can just be made out to the east of the village. Back at Derince, the metalled road continues eastwards to **Avtepe** (Ayios Symeon), the site of one of the largest rock tombs in Cyprus. This is visible from the road beyond the village, where it runs round opposite a cliff face: just past a little bridge about $1\frac{1}{2}$ miles after Avtepe (by the N62 road marker) the tomb, of impressive size and with an arched door and windows, can clearly be discerned some 500 ft (150 m) up the rampart-like cliff that girds the top of the ridge. Access to it is extremely difficult, but not impossible – Colin Thubron describes a successful ascent in 1972. The tomb is said to penetrate 87 ft (26 m) into the hill and to contain a great arched hall with side aisles and a well shaft of immense depth.

The surface of the road here is surprisingly good and the countryside hilly and varied. More ruined settlements and cave tombs from innumerable vanished civilizations dot the hillsides and the shore. Four miles ($6\frac{1}{2}$ km) on, **Kuruova** is an original Turkish village and has been largely unchanged by the events of the last three decades. South of the village the ruins of the massive Middle Bronze Age fortress of **Nitovikla** stand on a cliff overlooking the sea. The metalled road ends at another Turkish village, **Kaleburnu** (Galinporni), larger than Kuruova and picturesquely sited on the slopes of a hill honeycombed with rock-cut tombs, some of which have been incorporated within the houses. Not far off is another rock tomb of similar dimensions to that of Avtepe, beside the ruined church of Ayia Anna.

Bearing right onto a track before the main road turns inland towards Kaleburnu will bring you to another stretch of sand at Üsküdar (Scutari) Plaj; there is some oil and weed on the beach, and rocks below the waterline, but the place is adequate for a refreshing dip in the middle of the day. Minor roads lead from the steep and twisting streets of Kaleburnu to Dipkarpaz and Yenierenköy, but in a hired car it is wiser to return to Ziyamet along the tarmac, where you turn right to resume the route.

Two miles further on lies **Yeşilköy** (Ayios Andronikos): the Turkish name means 'green village' and is appropriate, for bananas, tomatoes and fruit trees grow in the red earth all around. Soon afterwards, the north coast comes into view for the first time and the road enters the sizeable village of **Yenierenköy** (Yialousa), boasting a petrol station, a hospital and a large school. The population today consists largely of resettled refugees from the 'red enclave' of Erenköy (Kokkina), the small patch of North Cyprus isolated beyond the Attila Line in the far west (*see p. 118*). The church is originally 13th century, with a large 18th-century building added on. North of Yenierenköy on **Yassi Burnu** (Cape Plakoti) is the public beach, reached down a track to the left after leaving the village; here there are facilities and a restaurant, and good bathing from gently shelving sand and flat rocks. Sea daffodils grow in profusion, and turtles use the beach for nesting.

Due east of Yenierenköy is **Sipahi**, whose exceptionally friendly inhabitants are mainly Turks from the Trabzon and Samsun regions of the mainland. The village is reached by

Detail of a mosaic at Ayias Trias

turning right before Yenierenköy is entered, and following this road round to the left after traversing Sipahi brings you to the site of the ruined early Christian basilica of **Ayias Trias** about a mile further on, marked by an ancient abandoned bus. A quantity of 6th-century mosaic paving survives in the three aisles (where the builder's name, Iraklios, can be read) and the remains of the baptistry can be seen, with the marble steps which led down to the font. The road past the basilica continues to rejoin the coast road, having bypassed Yenierenköy.

Beyond Yenierenköy, the next settlement is **Ayios Thyrsos**, no more than a hamlet consisting of a church and a restaurant: two churches, in fact, for besides the modern structure there is a ruined medieval church on the shore below. It contains traces of frescoes and an underground chamber reached by a flight of steps; some believe the vestigial caves nearby may have served as a third, even earlier place of worship. The coast here is of flat limestone pavements, good for swimming though seas can run high, and just beyond the hamlet is **Teresa Beach**, a tiny area of sand with four rather bedraggled umbrellas.

About 2 miles (3 km) further on a rough track leads south past rows of beehives, straight towards the tiny 10th-century church of **Ayios Photios tis Selinias**. The church has been used as a cowshed for some years but nevertheless faint traces of frescoes remain in places and a piece of a classical column is jammed into one of the walls.

The wide sweep of **Ronnas Bay** is now before you and just under 5 miles (8 km) from Ayios Thyrsos another rough track heads into the forest from opposite a picnic area. This one terminates after about a mile at another small church, the early 16th-century monastery church of the **Panayia Eleousa**, with a decorative southern doorway, sturdy vaulting within and small traces of frescoes visible behind the whitewash. The beach at Ronnas Bay is not accessible by car, but it can be reached on foot by any of several tracks.

The road now heads inland, snaking up the side of an intensively cultivated river valley to reach **Dipkarpaz** (Rizokarpaso), a large village of market gardens and smallholdings spread over a wide area of the plain. This village is unique in North Cyprus in that it is still home to a significant, though shrinking, community of Greek Cypriots (complete with a priest), supported by supplies brought by a UN lorry every Wednesday. Discussion of their presence is not welcomed, however, and they suffer from crippling restrictions. No Greek who visits the south is permitted to return, and, since children of over primary school age must go south if they are to receive education, the community's days seem numbered.

The imposing triple-aisled church of **Ayios Synesios** dominates the centre of the village. Built in the 12th century, it functioned under the Lusignans and Venetians as the cathedral of the Orthodox bishop of Famagusta, who was forced away from the city by a papal legate concerned to keep the Greek and Latin bishoprics apart, but the octagonal dome and the whole of the western end are 18th century. Orthodox services are held here every Sunday, but outside a statue of Atatürk asserts Turkish authority. Dipkarpaz was the capital of a province during the rule of the Lusignans and several important families had property here. In the past the women of the village were famous for their beauty, and several early travellers commented on the blue eyes and fair looks often seen among the people of the Kirpaşa peninsula. There is a petrol station in the village and two *pansiyons*, the Orhan and the Manastır.

At Dipkarpaz there is a choice of routes. A right turn by the church leads to the end of the peninsula, or one can head north to the coast to visit the sites of Carpasia and Aphendrika. Taking the former alternative first, the road winds south across the fertile plain, following signs to Zafer Burnu/Manastır, reaching the coast at **Khelones** where a Roman slipway lies beneath the water near some curiously shaped rocks. From here it follows the coast, to which a series of tracks of varying degrees of roughness lead from time to time. Three miles (5 km) from Dipkarpaz, by a small harbour, the Blue Sea Hotel has a restaurant and offers bed and breakfast for a little over £11 a night: it only has five rooms, however. Further along the coast, the Manastır restaurant has one double room to rent, and the Golden Beach restaurant a further two.

There is a surprisingly large amount of cultivated land in this remote extremity of Cyprus and for much of the year the landscape is pleasantly green, with small wooded hills and many flocks of sheep. The littoral alternates between small beaches and areas of flat rock right beside the road, until an enormous stretch of sandy beach is reached, backed by towering dunes with a small promontory at one end. This beach is said to be favoured by breeding turtles, and no wonder, for it is unpolluted, remote and only reachable on foot. Soon after passing it the tower of the **monastery church of Apostolos Andreas** appears on the far side of a rise and the Zafer (Klidhes) islands off the tip of Cyprus come into view.

The monastery here, 'the Lourdes of Cyprus', used to be crowded with pilgrims every weekend before 1974. St Andrew is said to have landed here on his way back to

The monastery of Apostolos Andreas

Palestine and restored the sight of his ship's captain by striking the rock where the monastery stands. Since then many more miracles have been recorded at the spot, some of them well authenticated: among the many tales of blindness cured and cripples restored after a night in the church, it is related that some thieves who broke into the church found the doors disappeared and themselves trapped inside: only when they returned the treasures they had stolen did the doors reappear, permitting them to escape. Another story tells of a mother who prayed to St Andrew to prevent her son from going to sea as a sailor: the saint heard her prayer and the boy stayed at home, only to be killed the following week in a road accident! In the 1960s the monastery enjoyed an annual income of several million pounds.

The church stands to one side of an enormous courtyard ringed with the small cells where pilgrims used to stay. A bored Turkish soldier will inspect your passport and copy its details into a log before handing you over to an elderly Greek gentleman, Andreas, who will open the church for you. The main church dates from 1740: its gilt iconostasis holds eight large icons and many smaller ones, but they are not of great interest. Some of the offerings brought by pilgrims are to be seen, often effigies in wax or silver of the part of the body for which they desired a cure. There are model ships here too, for St Andrew is a patron of seafarers. Nearer the sea is the original 15th-century Gothic chapel which may have been the crypt of the original church, a sad place today where an elderly Greek woman ponders the decline in the monastery's fortunes. She will give you a candle with which to peer through the extreme gloom at a handful of mouldering icons crammed into recesses in the walls, and will appreciate a little loose change for this service and being addressed in Greek. On the shore the rocks around an old jetty are littered with fragments of ancient masonry and three taps, once constantly in use for baptisms, drip neglected over their basin.

The monastery is where Isaac Comnenos finally surrendered to Richard the Lionheart in 1191 (*see p. 54*). Today it is occupied only by a handful of elderly Greeks and numerous cats, with a platoon of Turkish troops housed nearby. In one of the cells an enormous sow has taken up residence – whether her presence is meant to be a veiled insult to the occupying Muslims is unclear.

Leaving the immense square from the north-eastern corner, a good but unmetalled road heads towards **Zafer Burnu** (Cape Apostolos Andreas or Dinaretum); passing a flotsam-covered beach, three abandoned houses and a jetty, it reaches Cyprus' furthest point after some 4 miles (6½ km), a mere 60 miles (96 km) from Syria. The rocky mound on the Cape was the site of **Kastros**, one of the earliest settlements on the island; excavations in 1973 revealed circular huts (*tholoi*) of rubble, probably constructed around 7000 BC. Later a temple of Aphrodite stood here, but its stones were reused to build the monastery and only residual traces remain today on a plateau on the south side of the hill. The **Zafer Adaları** (Klidhes islands), lonely rocks beloved by seabirds, lie beyond the cape.

Alternatively, from Dipkarpaz centre bear left at the church and carry on uphill, bearing left at the top, then right; turn left at a T-junction and drive under the crumbling arch of a building that spans the road, then fork left to pass the 13th-century **church of Ayia Mavra**, once completely painted inside. Bear right here and soon Dipkarpaz is left behind and the north coast appears before you, with two modern buildings and the spectacular ruins of the **church of Ayios Philon** prominent on the lonely shore. Much of the rubble in the fields around is broken Roman pottery, for this was the site of ancient **Carpasia**, an important city in the Hellenistic and classical periods: it featured in Cypriot history when Demetrios landed here and occupied the city during the long period of strife following the death of Alexander the Great. Masonry from the ancient city was used to construct the 10th-century Byzantine church of Ayios Philon, to the south of which are the remains of a far earlier (possibly 5th-century) basilica which probably served as the cathedral of the early bishops of Carpasia (of

The 10th-century church of Ayios Philon, built within the earlier basilica

whom Philo, an important theologian, was the first, *c.* 401). The foundations and a simple circular mosaic floor can be seen. To the north, traces of the Roman harbour are clearly visible: the eastern mole still extends for some 379 feet (100 m) from the shore, and the recesses which once held the iron keys which clamped the stone blocks together can be easily discerned. Palm trees give this atmospheric site a Middle Eastern look, the few derelict buildings around the church serving only to add to its forlorn beauty. Carpasia was finally destroyed by the Saracens in 802 AD and its ruins have since been overwhelmed by the sand.

Five miles (8 km) eastwards along the coast lie the ruins of **Aphendrika**, another ancient site which Strabo tells us was one of the six most important cities of Cyprus *c.* 200 BC. The quality of the tarmac on this remote road shows that before 1974 the site was more visited than it is now. Today only three churches remain of the settlement. **Panayia Chrysiotissa**, the largest, is a 12th-century Romanesque structure, a huge building which must have existed for a comparatively short time before its destruction, for a smaller church was built within its walls in the 14th century. Nearby stand the ruins of a domed Byzantine church, **Ayios Georgios**, and a little way to the south another Romanesque church, **Panayia Asomatos**, with two very narrow arched passages connecting the three apses.

West of the churches is an extensive **necropolis**, with numerous tombs cut into the rock and very faint traces of a temple, and to the east, on top of a rocky outcrop, a primitive **citadel**. The lower parts of the rooms are carved out of the rock and are therefore still visible although the upper masonry has gone. To inspect the citadel, approach it from the south-east, where there is a wide passage. If time permits, there is much to explore here: about a mile to the north is the harbour, largely silted up, and some 1,500 metres along the shore is a beach, accessible through the fields.

The mole at Carpasia harbour, showing the slots in which lay the metal links holding the blocks together

FURTHER READING

General

Durrell, Lawrence, *Bitter Lemons* (London, 1957) the account of Durrell's years at Bellapais: funny, sad and a must for all visitors

Thubron, Colin, *Journey Into Cyprus* (London, 1975) the perceptive and readable account of a 600-mile walking tour throughout the island in 1972, a fascinating record of pre-partition Cyprus

Burch, Oliver, *The Infidel Sea* (Shedfield, Hants., 1990) a long and appreciative account of some months spent by an English family in the Republic, written at a time when military security was considerably tighter than it is today

History

Cobham, Claude Deval, *Excerpta Cypria: Materials for a History of Cyprus* (Cambridge 1908) a fascinating collection of extracts from 80 different writers from 23 AD to 1849 who either lived in Cyprus or visited it and recorded their impressions. A treasure trove for historians

Karageorgis, Vassos, *Cyprus: from the Stone Age to the Romans* (London, 1982) scholarly and thorough account of the ancient history of the island, with details of excavated sites

Luke, Sir Harry, *Cyprus Under the Turks* (Oxford, 1921, reprinted Lefkoşa, 1989) a readable survey of the contents of the British consular archives from the early 17th century on, reproducing many interesting documents and providing an insight into life during the Ottoman era (available from Rüstem's bookshop, Lefkoşa)

Morris, Jan, *The Venetian Empire* (London, 1980) chapter 5 is a rapid survey of Cyprus under the Venetians

Architecture

Gunnis, Rupert, *Historic Cyprus* (London, 1936, republished Lefkoşa, 1973) definitive descriptions of all the 1800 churches and monuments on Cyprus as they were in the 1930s by the then Inspector of Antiquities (available at Rüstem's bookshop, Lefkoşa, and despite its age a must for anyone interested in the architecture of the island)

Natural History

Bannerman, D.A., and Bannerman, M.W., *Birds of Cyprus* (London and Edinburgh, 1958)

Carter, David, *Butterflies* (London, 1988)

Halliday, Sonia, and Lushington, Laura, *Flowers of Northern Cyprus* (Lefkoşa, 1988)

Heinzel, H., Fitter, R.S.R., Parslow, J., *Birds of Britain and Europe with North Africa and the Middle East* (London, 1972)

Polunin, Oleg, *Trees and Bushes of Britain and Europe* (London, 1976)

Polunin, Oleg, and Huxley, Anthony, *Flowers of the Mediterranean* (n.e. London, 1987)

Other publications of specialist interest include Denktaş, R., *My Vision for Cyprus* (Lefkoşa, 1988); Dreghorn, W., *North Cyprus Bays and Beaches* (Lefkoşa, 1984); Heinze, C., *Cyprus Conflict* (Lefkoşa, 1986); Stylianou, A. and J., *The Painted Churches of Cyprus* (Lefkoşa, 1964), obtainable in London at Zeno's bookshop, Denmark St, London WC1; Turner, B.S., *The Story of the Cyprus Government Railway* (London, 1979); Westholm, A., *The Temples of Soli* (Stockholm, 1936).

INDEX AND GAZETTEER

surrounding pinewoods, much visited on summer weekends when the forests resound with music and the scent of barbecues overwhelms the aroma of pine and cistus; site of the North Cyprus herbarium (*qv*) 40, 76, 92, 93

Aşağı Bostancı (Kato Zhodia) sizeable agricultural village S of Güzelyurt and close to Attila Line 76, 118

Aşağı Dikmen (Kato Dhikomo) large village in southern Beşparmak foothills, reached from Lefkoşa or by mountain track from Bellapais; noted in the past for its handloom weaving 65, 95

ASIZ 31

Assyria 49, 134, 138

Aswan 143

Atatürk (Mustafa Kemal) father of modern Turkey 25, 61, 95, 115, 121, 131, 155

Atatürk Meydanı 10, 122, 126

Athens 49, 63, 115

Atlılar (Alodha) Mesarya village NW of Gazimağusa with many ruined houses: the Turkish inhabitants, together with those of nearby Murataga and Sandallar (*qqv*), were massacred and buried in a mass grave by EOKA B terrorists in 1974, and the village has its own garden of remembrance commemorating the victims

Attila Line 64, 114, 115, 118, 153

Augustus, Emperor 51, 143

Avtepe (Ayios Symeon) Turkish village on the Kirpaşa notable for an immense cave tomb in nearby cliff 152

Aydınköy (Prastio) village SW of Güzelyurt, with 18th-c church and nearby monastery of Ayios Nikolaos 114

Ayios Chrysostomos monastery the 'White Monastery' founded by Queen Helena Paleologos below Buffavento and marked by an enormous cypress tree; it has two adjacent Byzantine churches, the older restored but retaining a geometric marble floor and other details, the other 12th c with frescoes, both unfortunately

inaccessible within a military camp 91, 96

Ayios Mamas monastery well-preserved monastery church at Güzelyurt, originally Byzantine but reconstructed in Gothic style and built over an earlier temple of Aphrodite 76, 112–14

Ayios Philon *see* Carpasia

Ayios Photios tis Selinias 154

Ayios Thyrsos 154

Bafra (Vokolidha) village on Kirpaşa 15km NE of Boğaz, surrounded by ancient tombs; beach and uncompleted holiday village nearby 150

Bahçeli (Kalogrea) inland village on N slopes of mountains *c*.19 miles (30km) E of Girne 101

'Bambi beach' 107, 108

banks 24

Barnabas, St 51, 53, 145–6

baths 124, 133, 140, 141–2

beaches 12, 13, 14, 15, 16, 17, 34–5, 71–2, 74, 99–100, 104, 107, 108, 109, 112, 114, 117, 118, 136, 137–8, 140, 149, 150, 152, 153, 154, 155, 159

Bedesten 80, 125, 126

beer 19

Bellapais (Abbaye de la Paix) beautiful and spectacularly sited Gothic abbey 3½ miles (5km) SE of Girne, founded 1206 and much enlarged by Lusignan king Hugues III (1267–84); its abbots enjoyed special privileges, including the right to wear a mitre, but the abbey was plundered by Genoese and sank into obscurity (and moral laxity) under Venetians; 15, 21–2, 32, 55, 76, 77, 79, 87–90, 99 *see also* Beylerbeyi

belly dancing 23, 78

Berengaria of Navarre 54

Beşparmak (Trapeza) isolated village on N foothills of Mt Beşparmak 100

Beşparmak, Mt (Pentadaktylos) spectacular

peak (2429′, 740m) SE of Girne; its name, 'Five Fingers', reflects its shape which legend tells is the handprint of the hero Dighenis 91, 92, 100, 106

Beşparmak (Kyrenia) mountains   steep and 'Gothic' range of sharp peaks and romantic castles which divides the Mesarya plain from the north coast; its highest peak (Mt Selvili) is 3357′ (1023m) 1, 34, 35, 36, 37, 38, 39, 40, 41, 47, 53, 68, 73, 74, 94, 95, 96–8, 109, 110, 118, 150

Beylerbeyi (Bellapais)   village 3½ miles (5km) SE of Girne, named from and dominated by the abbey of Bellapais (*qv*); Lawrence Durrell's home from 1953–55 and celebrated in *Bitter Lemons* 87, 89–90

bicycles   9–10

birds   2, 41–2, 70, 91, 97, 107, 110, 112, 157

boat trips   77

Boğaz (Boghaz)   small traditionally Turkish fishing port and beach resort 15 miles (24km) N of Gazimağusa; gateway to Kirpaşa peninsula; many restaurants and two hotels 12, 13, 16, 22, 67, 68, 72, 77, 104, 149, 150

Boğaziçi (Lapathos)   village between Iskele and Geçitkale; immense Iron Age necropolis nearby 47

bookshops   79, 80, 122

Bragadino, Marco Antonio   58, 133

brandy sour   9

British   1, 40, 41, 54, 59, 60–1, 62, 63, 64, 66, 67, 75, 81, 88, 94, 96, 99, 107, 112, 119, 121, 122

British Commonwealth   61

British Council   75, 127

British Museum   109, 147

British Sovereign bases   30, 63, 130

Bronze Age   3, 47–9, 87, 94, 112, 146, 147, 152

Buffavento ('Wind-buffeted')   at 3100′ (945m) the loftiest of the 'Crusader castles' of the Beşparmak range, made impregnable by the sheer precipices on every side and tainted by an evil history; begun in 11th c and used mainly as a prison by the Lusignans – only Perot de Montolif ever escaped (by leaping off the crag onto a tree in 1385) and he did not live long thereafter; thoroughly dismantled by the Venetians, yet many inhabitants of Nicosia fled here from the Turks' advance; reached by a rough track and a steep climb on foot; little now remains of the (over 100) rooms in the castle and it is hard to picture the lay-out, but the dizzying views are stupendous 5, 53, 76, 77, 90–2, 95, 102, 103, 106

Bulla Cypria   55

buses   10–11, 121, 130

butterflies   2, 43, 91, 96, 97, 110

Büyük Han   123

Büyükkonuk (Komi Kebir)   village on a scenic route crossing the neck of the Kirpaşa peninsula and rounding the eastern flank of Kantara; centre of a fertile olive- and carob-growing area; ancient church of Ayios Auxentios, a German soldier turned hermit who lived in a nearby cave and is buried in a small chamber in the roof 104, 149, 150

Byzantines   3, 52–4, 59, 81, 82, 84, 85, 90, 93, 94, 96, 102, 107, 108, 112, 113, 119, 131, 138, 140, 141, 142, 145, 152, 158

cafés   77, 83, 85, 136, 146

Çamlıbel (Myrtou)   village 17 miles (27km) W of Girne; site of Late Bronze Age sanctuary and monastery of Ayios Pandeleimon, once the residence of the Orthodox bishop of Kyrenia, now within a military zone 39, 62, 111

camping 16–17, 150
Canbulat Bey 136
Canbulat Museum 75, 136
car hire 5, 7, 9–10, 32
carobs 53, 66, 101, 102
Carpasia important classical city
3 miles (5km) N of Dipkarpaz
and the first city taken by
Demetrios Poliorcetes, Ptolemy's
rival, in 306 BC; sacked by the
Saracens in 802 AD; Roman
harbour and ruined 10th-c
church of Ayios Philon built over
an earlier church of which a fine
mosaic pavement survives and
which was possibly the cathedral
of the See established under
Philo in 401 AD; Roman harbour
and Hellenistic and Roman
tombs 51, 53, 149, 155, 157–8,
159
carpets 68, 79, 80
cars 8–9
casinos 12, 13, 15, 78
castles 2, 5, 35, 39, 42, 53, 54,
55, 58, 62, 63, 71, 75, 76, 77, 79,
81–2, 83–6, 90–2, 95, 96, 102–3,
106, 119, 149, 150
Çatalköy (Ayios Epiktitos)
village popular with foreigners,
set on a ridge overlooking the sea
E of Girne; once famous for its
wood-carvers; 19th-c church
(mosque) on an earlier site
dedicated to German saint
(companion to Auxentios, *cf.*
Büyükkonuk) a hermit who lived
in a cave below the church 16,
22, 99
cathedrals 3, 55, 124–5, 131–2
Catholic Church 55, 59
caves 99, 152
Çayırova (Ayios Theodhoros)
Kirpaşa village set among
gardens and lemon trees, with
large modern mosque; the first
place in Cyprus to have a
telegraph office – an undersea
cable from Syria was laid under
the Ottomans; vestigial ruins of
ancient Cnidos, birthplace of
historian Ctesias, on coast 3 miles

(5km) to S 150
Çayönü (Kalopsidha)
agricultural Mesarya village near
Attila Line, 8 miles (13km) W of
Gazimağusa; once the most
powerful settlement in the E half
of the island; an important
middle Cypriot/Bronze Age site
was excavated to W of village in
1894 (the contents are now in the
Ashmolean); during the medieval
period owned by the Counts of
Jaffa but destroyed by the
Saracens in 1426; 2 churches, one
medieval, one 17th c; today many
of the houses are abandoned and
the enormous satellite dish of the
Dhekelia base looms to the S 47,
48
Cellarka complex of intricately
interlocked rock-cut tombs
constructed for the middle class
of Archaic Salamis, lying to S of
'Royal Tombs' (*qv*) 145
Charlotte, Queen 57
Chaucer 57
cheese 18, 22
children 13, 15, 16, 20
Christianity 51–2, 53, 83, 138,
141, 142
churches usually locked and
often converted into mosques;
determined enthusiasts should
apply to the Ministry of Tourism
or Education Ministry in Lefkoşa
regarding the possibility of
obtaining keys 3, 53, 58, 59, 78,
81, 82, 83, 85, 88, 92, 94, 95, 96,
99, 101, 102, 104–5, 109, 110,
111, 113–14, 115, 116, 117, 119,
123, 124, 126, 129, 130, 131, 133,
134, 136, 142, 143, 145–6, 150,
151, 152, 154, 155, 156, 157, 158
Cicero 50
Cilicia 50
citrus fruits 66, 108, 109, 112,
114, 115
Cleopatra 50
climate 2, 36–7
Cnidos classical city on coast S of
Çayırova (*qv*); minimal remains
150

doctors 27, 28

Doğancı (Elea)   broad river flowing from Troodos mts into Güzelyurt Bay 114

dolmuşes   10, 121

Dolphin Sailing   71, 74, 107

Dome Hotel   10, 13, 29, 77, 78, 81

Dörtyol (Prastio)   Mesarya village at junction of main Lefkoşa-Gazimağusa and Geçitkale–Larnaca roads (the name means crossroads); 2 miles S the remains of 14th-c Sigouris castle are visible to the left of the road – only a mound and faint outline of the moat remains, the fortress having been slighted by the Venetians and the remaining stones removed by the British for road-building

Drakos   Neolithic site near Serhadköy (*qv*) 46

driving   7–8, 111

Durrell, Lawrence   38, 87, 89, 99, 160

earthquakes   51, 52, 59, 131, 138, 140, 142

EC   65

Edict of Milan   52

Edremit (Trimithi)   village on road up to Karaman, with tiny Byzantine chapel of Panayia Khrysotrimithiotis forming the apse of a larger, later church 94, 107

Egypt   47, 48, 49, 50, 57, 60, 76, 95, 119, 129, 143, 146

Eleanor of Aragon   41, 84, 90

electricity   29–30, 62, 100

embroidery   79, 80, 83, 121

emergencies   27–8, 29, 31

Enkomi (Engomi, Engomi–Alasia)   ancient site near Salamis, inhabited from *c.*19th c BC; a major city and port and perhaps Cyprus' chief city with a large population swelled by Mycenaean immigrants, its true name is uncertain; abandoned early 11th c BC, when its population moved to Salamis; extensive ruins but not easy for the casual visitor to interpret 48, 49, 138, 143, 146–8, 149

enosis   61, 62, 63

EOKA   61, 63, 95, 104, 126

Ercan   TRNC's main airport, developed from the Tymbou airfield constructed by the British in the Second World War and opened 1975 4, 5–6, 7, 9, 12, 24, 67, 91

Erdemli (Tremethousha)   village W of Gazimağusa, where Richard I defeated Isaac Comnenos in 1191; its monastery of Ayios Spiridon is one of the largest and oldest in Cyprus; church (originally 7th c but rebuilt 18th c) is large with immense buttresses and an interior incorporating marble sarcophagi, Byzantine features and Gothic capitals from the earlier building; St Spiridon, the local bishop, was associated with numerous miracles, many of them after his death, when he became the much loved patron saint of Corfu; unfortunately the monastery complex now lies within a military camp and suspicion is shown if cameras are produced or any interest in the site displayed. Also inaccessible is the church of Ayios Photios, near the Line to the S, which may once have been a cathedral 51, 52

Erenköy (Kokkina)   coastal Turkish village now cut off from the rest of the TRNC by Greek Cypriot territory and occupied only by the army; its original inhabitants now live in Yenierenköy (*qv*) 62–3, 118, 153

Esentepe (Ayios Amvrosios)   sizeable village W of Girne, on Byzantine site: some houses retain tessellated floors of white stone; noted for apricots, weaving and wood-carving; large church with pepperpot domes and excellent but little visited sandy beach with bar and an abandoned hotel 28, 93, 94, 101

Eteocypriots   46, 49

Eusebius   49

Evagoras I   50, 138

Evelthon   138

excursions   76–7

Famagusta   *see* Gazimağusa

ferries   6

festivals   76

feudal system   55, 56

films   30, 75, 127

Fine Art Museum   75, 83

fish   18, 20, 21, 22, 45, 112, 150

fishing   45, 67, 104, 109, 150

flowers   2, 38–40, 74, 96, 109, 110, 143, 153

Folk Art Museum   75, 83

folk dancing   76

food   *see* cuisine

football   69

fortifications   3, 58, 82, 102, 119, 129, 134, 137, 152

Foscarini, Niccolo   135

fossils   107, 111

Frederick II   84

French   111, 119, 124

frescoes   83, 93–4, 102, 104–5, 110, 131, 134, 136, 142, 145, 151, 152, 154

fruit   66, 76, 108, 109, 112, 114, 115

galleries   75, 95

Galounia   ancient settlement on N coast at neck of Kirpaşa peninsula; possibly capital of Hittite kingdom of Cyprus; few remains visible 104

gambling   *see* casinos

Gazimağusa (Famagusta)   also called Mağosa (pop. 19,438); TRNC's second largest city and main port; founded in 3rd c BC by Ptolemy, one of Alexander's successors, and settled by refugees from Salamis (as Ammochostos – 'hidden by sand') but remained an obscure village until Henri II offered the area as a refuge for dispossessed Christians after the fall of Acre in 1291; town mushroomed thereafter, rapidly becoming one of the wealthiest cities on earth (with 365 churches) and a byword for wealth, worldliness and Levantine luxury until lost to the Genoese in 1373; architecture reflects the glories of the Lusignan period, while the fortifications display Venetian engineering at its most impressive; taken by the Turks after a famous siege in 1571, the walled city never recovered and remains an atmospheric 'bomb site' of ruined towers and crumbling structures of great beauty – 'one of the most remarkable ruins in the world' (H.V. Morton); most of the population live outside the walls 5, 6, 9, 10, 12–13, 15, 19, 22, 24, 26, 28, 29, 30, 31, 35, 36, 37, 38, 39, 41, 42, 55, 57, 58, 63, 66, 67, 69, 70, 71, 72, 75, 76, 77, 78, 79, 102, 104, 112, 129–37, 140, 142, 149, 151, 155 *see also* Maraş

Gaziveren (Ghaziveran)   Turkish village SW of Güzelyurt; the name ('Place of the Veterans') suggests it may have been founded by demobilized Turkish soldiers in the 16th c; object of an EOKA attack in 1964, when the villagers held off a large Greek force with a mere 12 rifles and only an ultimatum from Turkey stopped the fighting 114

Geçitkale (Lefkoniko)   large Mesarya village, centre of a peasants' revolt in 1472 and once famed for its lace, embroidery and striped weaving; several churches and a Roman temple site (much plundered) to S; TRNC's second airport lies nearby 28, 67, 105

Geçitköy (Panagra)   small village at W extremity of Beşparmak range; scenic gorge and reservoir nearby 111

Gemikonağı (Karavostasi, Xeros) the port of Soli (*qv*) and an important centre for the export of copper until the early 1970s; known as St Auxibios in Middle Ages and landing place of the Byzantine Helena Palaeologos, who married the Lusignan Jean II and did much to re-establish the status of the Orthodox Church against the Latin; today the port presents a scene of sad dereliction 68, 114, 115

Genoese 57, 81, 84, 90, 102, 125, 129

geology 34–6, 100, 104, 110, 112

Germans 60, 67, 68, 75, 94

Girne (Kyrenia) (pop. 7107) small northern port and tourist centre with famously pretty harbour dominated by powerful castle; founded (as Kerynia) in 10th c BC by Achaeans and became Corineum to the Romans; later walled against pirates and a centre for carob trade, but 'ruinous' in 1631 and by 1814 home to only a dozen families; revived under the British who improved the harbour and built the road to Lefkoşa; prior to 1974 a popular retirement town for expatriates, especially some 2500 British whose lives Lawrence Durrell humorously describes; now resettled by refugees from Limassol and once again resuming its role as genteel resort, with new harbour to E of town 5, 6, 9, 10, 12, 13–14, 15–16, 20–1, 24, 26, 28, 29, 31, 32, 34, 36, 54, 55, 58, 59, 60, 62, 67, 69, 70, 71, 72, 75, 76, 77, 78, 79, 80, 81–3, 94, 99, 102, 104, 106, 107, 149

Girne castle one of the best-preserved fortresses in the Levant; begun by the Byzantines, rebuilt by the Lusignans and massively reinforced by the Venetians; the object of many sieges but never taken by storm 75, 76, 79, 81–2

Girne Gate 121

Glapsides beach backed by wetlands N of Gazimağusa; good bird-watching 42, 137

golf 69, 114

Gönendere (Knodhara) Mesarya agricultural village W of Geçitkale 105

Gönyeli (Geunyeli) Turkish suburb on northern outskirts of Lefkoşa; from 1950s the stronghold of Rauf Denktaş' underground organisation Volkan (later the TMT) and scene of several bloody incidents; nearby reservoir good for bird-watching 42, 121

Greece 47, 60, 61, 62, 63, 118

Greek Cypriots 60, 61, 62, 64, 65, 95, 96, 99, 118, 130, 152, 154, 156, 157

Greeks 3, 48–9, 50, 105, 108, 117, 119

'Green Line' 62, 123, 127

Grivas, George ('Dighenis') 61, 63, 104, 118

Gulf War 1, 151

Güngör (Koutsovendis) once Maronite village in eroded landscape S of Buffavento; large ruined 12th-c church, but inaccessible since the whole village lies within a military zone 91, 96

Güzelyalı (Vavilas) small fishing village W of Girne 109

Güzelyurt (Morphou) (pop. 11,357) busy town 24 miles (38km) W of Lefkoşa; inhabited since the Bronze Age, a copper-mining centre and a barony in the medieval period; now the heart of an important fruit-growing (especially citrus and strawberries) area in the well-irrigated western plain; under the British, connected by railway to Nicosia and Famagusta; museum and monastery of Ayios Mamas (*qv*) 28, 31, 35, 38, 41, 46, 48, 63, 66, 76, 112–14, 118, 136

Güzelyurt (Morphou) Bay 34, 42, 112, 114, 117

gypsum 68

Hadrian, Emperor 52

handicrafts 78–80, 83, 105, 121

Haspolat (Mia Milea) village NE of Lefkoşa; so named by Greeks because it lies one Greek mile (3 English miles) from the capital

Hazreti Ömer Tekke (Ayii Phanontes) shrine on coast E of Girne, commemorating 7 Muslim holy men (possibly killed during a 7th-c raid), revered by Turkish and Greek Cypriots alike 99

Haydarpaşa Mosque 126

health *see* medical facilities, doctors

Hellenistic period 112, 115, 138

Henri I 84

Henri II 129

Herodotos 138

Hittites 48, 76, 101

Homer 138, 144, 145

horse-riding 13, 15, 70, 107

horses 15, 47, 70, 107, 144, 145

hospitals 28, 83, 99, 114

hotels 12–14, 67, 72, 77, 78, 81, 83, 99, 104, 107, 108, 109, 122, 127, 136, 149, 150, 155

Hugues III 57, 88, 125

Hugues IV 57

hunting 42, 70

Icon Museums 75, 83, 104, 146

icons 75, 83, 95, 104, 145, 146, 156

Ilgaz village on northern slopes of Beşparmak mts, scheduled for refurbishment in style of Karaman (*qv*) 94

immigration 46, 47, 48–9, 64

Incesu (Elea) small village S of Alsancak; church of Ayios Nikolaos incorporates a late 15th-c tombstone showing a lifesize man in armour; slight remains of medieval buildings; good walking

Incirli (Makraskya) village W of Gazimağusa and S of Köprülü, close to Attila Line and British Dhekelia base; an important place in Middle Ages; several ruined churches of 12th–16th c, and remains of many medieval buildings

industry 67–8, 112, 114

inflation 12, 25

Inönü (Sinda) small Turkish village reached across a bleak section of the plain NE of Vadili; large Late Bronze Age enclosure nearby with cyclopean stone walls and Mycenaean acropolis of *c*.1500 BC; a Genoese army was surprised here after sacking Nicosia by a Lusignan sortie from Kyrenia

insects 43–4

insurance 7

Iskele (Trikomo) large village N of Gazimağusa; birthplace of EOKA leader George Grivas (*qv*) and famous for its pomegranates; delightful small chapel of Ayios Iakovos in central square, incorporating porcelain plates in roof vaulting; larger 12th-c Panayia Theotokos, with frescoes, now functions as an icon museum 28, 39, 75, 104–5

Islam 26, 46, 53, 125

Istanbul 4, 5, 6, 68

Izmir 4, 5, 68

Jacques I 102

Jacques II 57, 131

Jacques III 131

Jerusalem 53, 54, 55, 87, 88, 131, 135

jewellery 79, 117, 133, 147, 148

Jews 51–2, 138

Joanna of Sicily 54

John, Prince of Antioch 84, 86, 102

Justinian II 53

Kakozonara quarries 151

Kaleburnu (Galinporni) Moslem village on Kirpaşa, set on hillside riddled with rock tombs, some of them incorporated into the houses; immense rock-cut tomb chamber 69' (21m) long with deep side chambers (*cf.* Avtepe) lies near village, now used as a stable; sandy beach nearby 47, 152

Kalecik (Gastria) Kirpaşa village, with faint remains of a castle built by the Templars in 1191 and destroyed by Hugues III in 1278; rock-cut cisterns on a promontory looking over the sea, and ruined chapel of St John by the shore; mosaic cubes lying around suggest there may once have been a large Byzantine church here; today the site of the TRNC's oil terminal and cement works 68, 150

Kalkanlı (Kalokhorio) agricultural village on a ridge N of Güzelyurt, with fine views of the plain; large 19th-c church incorporates an earlier (16th-c) building as its S aisle 98, 112

Kanakaria *see* Panayia Kanakaria

Kanli Dere (Pedhieos) major river watering the Mesarya plain and reaching the coast at Enkomi 124, 146, 147

Kantara easternmost of the castles on the Beşparmak range; though slighted by Venetians and abandoned in 1525, much of the outer fortifications are preserved; dramatic views from 2300' (700m) up 39, 42, 54, 55, 76, 92, 102–3, 149, 150

Kaplıca (Dhavlos) village near N coast at neck of Kirpaşa peninsula, with a dominant white mosque; a Late Cypriot site; small fishing harbour with shingle beach, an abandoned hotel and, to W of the village, a broad stretch of soft golden sand with facilities but few visitors 36, 104

Karaağaç (Kharcha) inland village E of Girne; 19th-c church with unusual pebble floor 93, 101

Karageorghis, Vassos 49, 160

Karakum (Karakoumi) small village near Girne; several restaurants and a small sandy beach 14, 22, 99

Karaman (Karmi) picturesque mountain village S of Karaoğlanoğlu, largely inhabited by British and German expatriates who have renovated and gentrified the quaint old houses; the mountains rising steeply to the south make Karaman cool in summer, but in winter it scarcely sees the sun (though clear views across to the Taurus mountains and the green hillsides around compensate); restaurants, art gallery, crafts shop and a pub 21, 32, 40, 79, 86, 94–5, 97, 107

Karaoğlanoğlu (Ayios Georgios) extensive village W of Girne; once known as 'Tiger Bay', the beach to W of the village was the landing place of Turkish army in 1974 16, 25, 63, 70, 75, 77, 78, 79, 94, 107, 130

Karpas *see* Kirpaşa

Karpaşa (Karpasha) Maronite village near a forest, reached by a left turn in Çamlıbel; its church (a 20th-c restoration on a medieval site) is locked and symbolically dominated by Çamlıbel's looming minarets, and the dwindling Maronite population shows signs of being overwhelmed by mainland immigrants

Karpasia *see* Carpasia

Karşıyaka (Vasilia) village on northern foothills of Mt Kıvanç W of Girne; derelict monastery above and Bronze Age necropolis around; good walking 98, 109

Kastros Neolithic site at extreme tip of Zafer Burnu 46, 157

Kayalar (Orga) small and

population relocated to Lapta (*qv*); Roman fishtanks visible by the shore, Franco-Byzantine church and rock-hewn chapel where the 'Lambousa Treasure' was found; but all inaccessible within a military encampment 89, 108–9

Nicephoras Phocas 53

Nicocreon 138, 148

Nicosia see Lefkoşa

night clubs 77–8

nightlife 77–8

Nitovikla ruined Middle Bronze Age fortress on a cliff S of Kuruova; this massive rectangular fort, built to an Anatolian or Syrian design, was constructed to defend the Kirpaşa against seaborne raiders, already a threat as early as 1700 BC 47, 152

Nores, Louis de 123

North Cyprus Herbarium 92, 93

oil 51, 150

olives 66

Ortaköy (Orta Keuy) described in the 1930s as 'a miserable Turkish hamlet' and today an unattractive suburb to N of Lefkoşa, with factories and apartment blocks; like nearby Gönyeli a TMT stronghold in the 1960s 78, 121

Orthodox Church 53, 55, 59, 146, 155

Othello Tower 76, 129, 135–6

Ottomans 3, 57, 58, 59–60, 81, 82, 123

Ozanköy (Kazaphani) traditional Turkish village 3 miles (5km) SE of Girne, dominated by the squat minaret of its mosque, originally a frescoed medieval church and containing a well-preserved wall tomb depicting a man in 14th-c dress; a stream runs through the village under several bridges and past the Old Mill restaurant 22

Özhan (Asomatos) once-Maronite village on the Çamlıbel–Lefkoşa road; now, like several neighbouring villages, occupied by the military

Paleokastro Bronze Age site on coast near Akdeniz (qv);

inaccessible within military zone 48, 111

Palestine 46, 49, 51, 56, 129, 156

Pamuklu (Tavros) Kirpaşa village between Çayırova and Kumyalı 150

Panayia Absinthiotissa remote monastery on S slopes of the mountains near Kaynakköy; owned by the Orthodox See of Jerusalem and known as the Abbey of Abscithi in the Middle Ages; Byzantine church with later Gothic vaulting and well-preserved narthex 95–6

Panayia Eleousa remote monastery inland from Ronnas Bay 154

Panayia Kanakaria beautiful and well-preserved monastery church near Boltaşlı (Lythrangomi) on the Kirpaşa, 33 miles (53km) NE of Gazimağusa; 11th-c rebuilding of a 6th-c basilica with 12th and 18th-c additions; contained miraculous içons and a celebrated 5th-c mosaic, the appearance of which on the international art market after 1974 aroused concern 151–2

Panayia Melandryna 15th-c monastery church near Esentepe, repaired in 18th c when heavy flying buttresses were added; said to stand on the site of a pagan temple; nearby classical necropolis 101

Panayia Pergamiotissa medieval domed monastery church on coast c. 3 miles (5km) from Tatlisu; surrounded by ancient fragments with nearby rock-cut chapel 102

pansiyons 12, 14, 149, 155

Paphos 51, 62, 138, 151

Paşaköy (Asha) Mesarya village between Ercan and Vadili; remains of the Salamis–Kythrea aqueduct beside the road; owned by the noble de Nores family under the Lusignans and was the site of a Venetian council of war after the Turkish invasion of 1570; the local speciality is brick-making

wealth from nearby copper mines made it one of the most important cities on the island for a millennium; strongly anti-Persian, but prospered once more in the Hellenistic and Roman periods, when it may have boasted the first public library in the world; abandoned 7th c but became the seat of the Orthodox bishop of Nicosia under the Lusignans; the remains visible today are Roman: a basilica with mosaic floors, agora and reconstructed 2nd-c AD theatre; considerable ruins survived in the 18th c but the British took much of its stone to Egypt; some say the citizens' sloppy speech provides the origin of the word 'solecism' 34, 49–50, 51, 68, 76, 77, 115–17

Solon 49, 115

Sourp Magar monastery lying N of forest road to Alevkaya; a Coptic foundation *c*.1000, but handed to the Armenians in the 15th c and used as a resting point for pilgrims to the Holy Land; present ruins are 19th-c with medieval fragments 92–3

Spain 49

Spartans 108

Spiridon, St 52 *see also* Erdemli

sport 69–74

squash 71

'St Catherine's Prison' 144–5

Strabo 158

Suez Canal 60, 117, 130

supermarkets 15, 16, 107

Sütlüce (Psilatos) Mesarya village W of Geçitkale; settled since the Middle Bronze Age 47, 105

swimming 71–2 *see also* beaches

Syria 34, 46, 47, 102, 119, 124, 134

taksim 63, 64

Taşkent (Vouno) once Maronite village N of Lefkoşa, below a hillside emblazoned with the North Cypriot flag; 16th-c monastery and cave nearby with fossil bones; martyrs' museum 95

Taşlıca (Neta) settlement on E coast of Kırpaşa, with ruins of a large temple to E and numerous terracotta fragments in fields to S; 18th-c church has ancient vaulted chamber beneath and holy well 152

Taşucu 6

Tatlısu (Akanthou) substantial inland village E of Girne; immense modern church/mosque; beaches on the nearby coast of pebble, sand and flat rocks, usually deserted by all but seabirds 34, 101

taxis 6, 10, 137

Telamon 138

telephones 12, 26–7

television 30

Tell el-Amarna 146

temples 3, 110, 111, 113, 116, 117, 143, 148, 152, 157

tennis 12, 13, 15, 16, 72–3

Tepebaşı (Dhiorios) village enjoying commanding position over Güzelyurt Bay, founded 7th/8th c BC; noted in different eras for its embroidery, cheese and woodworking; early 19th-c church of Ayia Marina on an ancient site 111

terrorism 62, 95, 114, 115, 121, 127

Teucer 49, 138

theatres 74, 75

theatres, Roman 51, 116, 142

Theseus 115

Thubron, Colin 152, 160

Tillyria 114

time 24

tipping 29

TMT (Türk Müdafa Teşkilatı) Turkish Cypriot resistance movement which succeeded Rauf Denktaş' 'Volcan' in 1957 61, 127

tobacco 66

tombs 83, 94–5, 100, 109, 115, 121, 122–3, 132, 144–5, 146, 147,